D

Twayne's United States Authors Series

Sylvia E. Bowman, *Editor*

INDIANA UNIVERSITY

E. E. Cummings

 46

E. E. Cummings

by BARRY A. MARKS

Brown University

TWAYNE PUBLISHERS

A DIVISION OF G. K. HALL & CO., BOSTON

MANUFACTURED IN THE UNITED STATES OF AMERICA

To BHS

Contents

About the Author

Born in New York City in 1926, Barry A Marks was graduated from Deerfield Academy, received an A.B. from Dartmouth College, and M.A. and Ph.D. degrees from the University of Minnesota. He has taught as well as studied at Dartmouth and Minnesota, and since 1955 has been a member of the English Department at Brown University. He edited a volume of Mark Twain criticism for the Amherst American Civilization series (*Mark Twain's Huckleberry Finn.* 1959) and published articles in *American Quarterly, Nineteenth Century Fiction,* and *The English Journal* in addition to various scholarly and quasi-scholarly activities for local journals and TV.

Preface

E. E. CUMMINGS created poems, plays, novels, ballets, and paintings steadily from 1922 until his death in 1962. His work has been widely and favorably reviewed. Articles in learned journals have scrutinized him. Several doctoral theses have examined him microscopically. A book in 1960 accorded him a full-scale treatment. Although the scholar's interest in Cummings has not approached that evinced in his contemporaries, T. S. Eliot or William Faulkner, Cummings scholarship is unusual in that its quality is high and the degree of consensus about the subject is remarkable. What need, then, for a new opinion?

In the first place, scholars know Cummings the way child psychologists know children. They know a great deal about his work as a whole, but they know very little about individual works. If there is a difference between Cummings experts and child experts, it is that child experts are more likely to realize that children are more interesting than the generalizations about them. A sufficient number of poems have been discovered, however, so that Cummings' most ardent admirers know that miracles await further exploration. The way is open, therefore, and will be for some time to come, for any new study which can illumine Cummings' intentions and the way they are embodied in individual poems.

In the last quarter century, during which the United States has made enormous contributions to the world's poetry, as well as the other arts, E. E. Cummings has stood as a leading figure with T. S. Eliot, Robert Frost, and Wallace Stevens. Yet he remains relatively unknown, even among the college educated. To be sure, he often makes exceedingly stringent demands upon his readers. But these demands reflect his search for a contemporary language with which to speak significantly to the men and women of the twentieth century. The present study assumes that Cummings' poetry well rewards whatever effort may be required to understand and respond deeply to it, and the assumption has largely determined the shape of this book.

The Bibliography lists one book and several articles which have analyzed, classified, and generalized about Cummings' subjects and ideas and techniques and, to some extent, his place in the history of poetry. The primary intent of this new study is to approach Cummings' work from the inside, inductively, as it were: to give careful attention to a relatively small number of poems. It means, generally speaking, consideration of whole poems rather than selected lines and stanzas. It means sacrificing comprehensiveness in the interests of concentration.

Chapter 1 analyzes four poems. The assumption is that there is little profit to be gained from talking *about* a poet before meeting him. Thus, the first chapter permits four poems simply to lead where they will, with little regard for large-scale description of the poet or the total body of his work.

The remaining chapters analyze Cummings' poetic achievement from a series of highly restricted points of view. Chapters 2 and·3 treat Cummings' interest in children and sex. Other subjects might have been chosen, such as nature, politics, science and technology, education, religion, or travel. No claim is made that children and sex loom larger or stand closer to the center of Cummings' work than other subjects; the only claim is that a close look at these subjects can lead both deeply into the poet's basic sense of life and broadly into his attitudes and judgments concerning many other matters.

Chapters 4 and 5, which should be read as a single essay, analyze Cummings' conception of art, his own and that of contemporaries working in many different media. Cummings is a peculiarly instructive figure, not only because he is a fine poet, but also because he is a highly representative modern artist. From his undergraduate days at Harvard until his death, he maintained a thoroughly adulterous relationship with a variety of art forms other than poetry. He was participant, observer, critic, and just plain lover of everything from the painting of Cezanne and Marin, the sculpture of Gaston Lachaise, and the music of Stravinsky, to the comic strips of George Harriman and the teasing strips of June St. Clare. The result of all this cross-fertilization is apparent in his poetry; thus an understanding of Cummings' relationship to contemporary art in general can illuminate both contemporary art and Cummings' poems.

Chapter 6 examines Cummings' response to his native land. The intent is to characterize Cummings by observing the way in which his work both criticizes and evokes American culture. Few artists today wish to be thought of in narrowly nationalistic terms. The dangers of parochialism are all too apparent. At the same time, however, Cummings was acutely aware of his country, its relation to European culture, its peculiar strengths and weaknesses. The sixth and final chapter therefore assesses Cummings as an *American* poet.

One final word of introduction, and a personal one at that. One who professes to admire Cummings and who, therefore, sets out to share his admiration with others finds himself in a highly ambiguous position. He knows that many people find Cummings' poetry uninteresting or unintelligible, or both. He thinks that others would profit from looking at the poetry in ways which may not have occurred to them. He determines, therefore, to set forth certain insights which he values in the hope that others may read Cummings with richer pleasure and understanding.

On the other hand, he knows also that few artists have attacked critics with as devastating blows as did E. E. Cummings. It was a moment of unusual restraint when he referred to them as Gentlemen Dealers in Second Hand Thoughts. But the difficulty for a Cummings critic is not merely that the poet might have disapproved. The problem is deeper and more interesting than that, for Cummings' objection to criticism was central to everything he represented. Critics murder the art they write about, he thought. No matter how good the criticism, its inherent tendency is to short-circuit and, thus, to mar the relationship between reader and poem.

A poem is not an idea. It is an experience, a carefully shaped experience in which a reader may discover something about life, the author, and himself. And E. E. Cummings prized experience and discovery even more than most poets. No wonder, then, that he felt his art threatened by the onslaughts of criticism. And no wonder that an admirer should wish, somehow, both to speak and to remain silent.

To put the problem another way, a poem is a little like a joke: a listener does not really understand a joke until he has laughed; yet who can laugh with anything like equal heartiness at a joke and an explanation of it? To explain and not to explain is, thus, a fundamental ambiguity at the root of this book. Since it seems unresolvable, perhaps the most that can be done is to acknowledge that it exists, partly as a warning to readers, partly as obeisance to one of the great spirits of our time.

While no one but me is responsible for errors of fact or judgment, I wish to record my particular thanks to several of the many people who have contributed to the writing of this book. Wells B. Grogan has helped far more than he realizes. So has Albert D. Van Nostrand, from whom I learned to read. Criticizing the manuscript is only the most recent service done me by two friends and colleagues, Hyatt H. Waggoner and David R. Weimer. I am grateful for the editorial work of Sylvia Bowman. I owe thanks also to my wife Gale for her critical judgment as well as for her patience.

BARRY A. MARKS

Brown University

Acknowledgments

Harcourt, Brace & World, Inc. has kindly given permission to quote both from *Poems 1923-1954, 95 Poems,* and *Eimi* by E. E. Cummings and from "Dry Salvages" in *Four Quartets* by T. S. Eliot.

Robert Littell has given permission to quote from his review of *The Enormous Room,* which appeared in *The New Republic.*

Charles Norman and the Macmillan Company have given permission to quote from *The Magic-Maker.*

"in Just":
> Copyright, 1923, 1951 by E. E. Cummings. Reprinted from his volume POEMS 1923-1954 by permission of Harcourt, Brace & World, Inc.

"O sweet spontaneous":
> Copyright, 1923, 1951, by E. E. Cummings. Reprinted from his volume POEMS 1923-1954 by permission of Harcourt, Brace & World, Inc.

"raise the shade":
> Copyright, 1925, by E. E. Cummings. Reprinted from his volume POEMS 1923-1954 by permission of Harcourt, Brace & World, Inc.

"i will be":
> Copyright, 1925, by E. E. Cummings. Reprinted from his volume POEMS 1923-1954 by permission of Harcourt, Brace & World, Inc.

"the skinny voice":
> Copyright, 1925, by E. E. Cummings. Reprinted from his volume POEMS 1923-1954 by permission of Harcourt, Brace & World, Inc.

"who knows if the moon's":
> Copyright, 1925, by E. E. Cummings. Reprinted from his volume POEMS 1923-1954 by permission of Harcourt, Brace & World, Inc.

"Marj":
> Copyright, 1926, by Horace A. Liveright; renewed, 1954 by E. E. Cummings. Reprinted from his volume POEMS 1923-1954 by permission of Harcourt, Brace & World, Inc.

Acknowledgments

Chronology

1894 E.E. Cummings, born October 14, Cambridge, Massachu-
setts, son of Edward Cummings, a Harvard professor
(later, a Unitarian minister), and Rebecca Haswell
Clarke.

1912 First published poem in *Harvard Monthly*.

1915 Graduated from Harvard, *magna cum laude*. Delivered
Commencement Address, "The New Art."

1916 Received M.A. from Harvard.

1917 June: joined Norton Harjes Ambulance Corps, American
Red Cross, in France. September-December: imprisoned
by French authorities for merely loving France and not
also hating Germany and for lacking "illimitable respect"
for bureaucratic procedures.

1920 First major appearance as a poet in the first issue of the
resurrected publication, *The Dial*.

1921– First sojourn in Paris, including second trip to a French
1923 jail (duration: a few hours). Cummings lived in Paris
intermittently throughout the 1920's and made at least
five trips abroad thereafter.

1922 Publication of *The Enormous Room*, based on experiences
of 1917.

1923 Publication of first volume of poetry, *Tulips and
Chimneys*.

1925 Received The Dial Award for "distinguished service to
American letters." Publication of *&(And)* and *XLI Poems*.

1928 Production of *Him* at the Provincetown Playhouse.

1930 Production of ———, a collection of nonsense essay-fairy
tales, a book without a title.

1931 Trip to Russia (see *Eimi*). First major showing of paintings: twenty-nine pictures exhibited at the Painters and Sculptors Gallery. Publication of *CIOPW*, a collection of works done in charcoal, ink, oil, pencil, and watercolor. Also: *VV(ViVa)*.

1935 Publication of *Tom*, a ballet based on *Uncle Tom's Cabin*. Although never staged, David Diamond composed a complete score for it. Publication also of *No Thanks* (to the fourteen named publishers, that is, who would not print the book and with thanks to his mother who did).

1949 One man show of paintings, American British Art Centre.

1950 Awarded Fellowship of the Academy of American Poets for "great achievement." Publication of *XAIPE*.

1952– Charles Eliot Norton lecturer at Harvard (see *i: Six*
1953 *Nonlectures*).

1954 Publication of *Poems 1923-1954*.

1955 Awarded special citation by National Book Awards for *Poems 1923-1954*.

1957 Received Bollingen Prize in Poetry and Boston Arts Festival Poetry Award.

1959 One man show, Rochester Memorial Art Gallery.

1962 Died, September 3, North Conway, N. H.

E. E. Cummings

Four Poems

I · "l(a"

IN 1958 E. E. Cummings published his twelfth and last
volume of poetry, 95 *Poems*. The first poem in the collection
looked like this:

```
l(a

le
af
fa

ll

s)
one
l

iness
```

More like a picture of the Washington Monument or a telephone
pole than a poem, it shocked even those who had had a long
acquaintance with Cummings' work. To those who were not old
friends, it seemed stupid. It frustrated. It confirmed convictions
about the uselessness of art in general and of modern art in
particular. It didn't say anything.

The reaction is understandable. But the poem deserves attention. If for no other reason, a respected poet determined to
introduce his last book with it. On the other hand, deciding to
look at the poem carefully should not lead us to reject totally
our first impression. Indeed, the shock of its appearance on the
page and the lack of any recognizable statement are very impor-

tant. The poem contrasts sharply with the firm-packed, box-like appearance of a fourteen-line sonnet. And far from asserting anything so obviously poetical as "My love is like a red, red rose," far even from saying something which sounds like prose but which at least looks like poetry, such as:

> Home is the place where, when you have to go there,
> They have to take you in.

Cummings' whole poem is less than a complete sentence, and the individual words appear to have been in a serious accident.

Whatever else he did, Cummings calculated first impressions. He made certain assumptions about his readers, and he issued a warning. He said, "Watch out! This poem is not for the faint-hearted. It will not yield to those who merely want their prejudices caressed. Open up!"

At the same time, however, Cummings offered even to the first impression something more than mere rebellious anti-traditionalism. If the poem is nothing like most poems, it clearly has a form of its own. It might have spattered the page like the pieces of a mirror dropped on the floor. In fact, it is neat and even orderly. Furthermore, the "lines" are symmetrically patterned into "stanzas" of one and three lines alternately: 1-3-1-3-1.

These observations concern the poem's surface only, and they are both as important and as unimportant as what we can glean from a man's face at first meeting. First impressions may be misleading, but they will never be wholly contradicted. For better or for worse, this poem's appearance suggests a new experience which, nevertheless, has shape and meaning.

But how do we approach the meaning of a poem which does not clearly *say* anything? Cummings'. poem presents immediately the formidable problem which confronts the audiences of all the contemporary arts. Novels do not tell stories; paintings do not depict; music is not melodic. In a significant way, however, the problem is not limited to the contemporary arts, for modern science is in a similar fix. Science no longer even asks questions about the real nature of the physical world, for it knows the world is too complicated for that. It asks rather about the patterned way in which known particles are moving in a particular object. Thus even as commonplace a thing as a table is, for modern science, at best a highly predictable pattern of moving electrons. In like fashion, a useful way of avoiding—at least temporarily—the frustrating question, "What does the poem say?" is to ask instead, "What is the poem made of and how is it arranged?"

Cummings' poem consists of two large elements: the word "loneliness" and the parenthetical interjection, "a leaf falls." A parenthesis normally adds to a sentence an explanatory comment which the writer wants held in mind at the same time that he completes his main idea. So, here, Cummings asks that we hold in mind simultaneously the idea of loneliness and the image of a leaf falling. He might have said, "Loneliness is like a falling leaf." More specifically, he might have said, "The feeling of loneliness is the feeling a man gets when he watches a single leaf falling." It does not take much imagination to fill in around this assertion and think of autumn, the end of the growing season, the death of the year.

But Cummings' poem does not make an assertion about loneliness. Such an assertion would not have been very interesting. We would have nodded or shaken our heads, according to our inclination, and gone about more important business. Instead, the poem combines the abstract idea and the concrete image in such a way as to show us something and, in showing us, to elicit our participation in a meaningful experience. It asks us, in effect, not to cogitate about the relationship between loneliness and dead leaves and, if we wish, to make our own poem; it asks us to look at the printed page.

What extra dividends does Cummings declare by his apparently whimsical splitting of the word "loneliness"? Omitting the parenthesis, the poem looks like this:

l
one
l
iness

Thanks to the modern typewriter whose letter "el" (1) doubles as the figure one (1), Cummings shows us that a very commonplace word is really a quite singular word. It states its meaning five times. It says, "loneliness," but it also says, "one-one-one-iness" (that is, the quality or condition of being "I"). Cummings has revealed something quite extraordinary in a word we had always thought very ordinary. This is a discovery. It is difficult to say how valuable a discovery it is, but it is one of a special kind.

Most linguistic discoveries have to do with meaning. Teen-agers in the 1930's, for example, used the word "hot" to refer to the kind of music they liked and then extended it to designate anything they liked. The same thing happened to "cool" in the 1950's. Franklin Roosevelt added a subtle dimension to the meaning of "fear" in his announcement "The only thing we have to fear is fear itself." But Cummings' treatment of "loneliness" adds to the word not a semantic quality but what critics of the visual arts call a "plastic quality." He does not deepen or extend its meaning in any way; it has suddenly become vital to the touch, as it were, and has become an object of delight.

The arrangement of the parenthetical material in the poem likewise yields special plastic values. Its verticality is a linguistic picture of the falling leaf. Even the letters have visual import. The pattern of large and small letters in "le/af/fa/11" suggests the graceful, delicate twisting of the leaf as it circuitously falls. The single letters at the beginning and the end of the process ("a....s") enclose four two-letter lines, and, in so doing, reveal an overall symmetry in the leaf's falling and, at the same time, echo the symmetrical stanza arrangement of the poem as a whole.

In addition to visual effects the poem gains significant sound values from breaking up and rearranging the words.[1] The visual twisting of the leaf benefits from being bound together by sound. A long "e" binds the movement from "le" to "af." The "f" does the same for the next two lines. More important, however, are the thrust and resolution produced by Cummings' handling of the only repeated sounds: "l," "e," and "s." The "l" in "leaf" echoes the first "l" in "loneliness" and aids the process of holding in mind simultaneously the material within and without the parenthesis. It is emphasized by the double "l" in "falls" just before the parenthesis ends, when the reader returns to the development of "loneliness." In like fashion, the final "s" in "falls," at the end of the parenthesis, points toward the double "s" at the very end of the poem.

The last line "iness" resolves the poem in several ways. It not only rounds out the "s" in "falls" but, in doing so, repeats another sound from the parenthetical phrase, the "e" in "leaf." With its two syllables it is also a long line, befitting a conclusion. Its "rhyme," its length, together with the whispering quality of the "s" sound itself, combine to suggest effectively the settling of the fallen leaf. The line, in short, provides a synthesizing final chord for both the sounds and the action of the poem, just as it completes the tortuous route of the word "loneliness" itself.

This analysis of the development of Cummings' poem implies surprising conclusions. The poem is quite different from the sentimental self-pity in which we might have indulged ourselves if we had simply sat back and contemplated the identity of a falling leaf and loneliness and the evanescence and meaninglessness of life. Man is indeed as fragile as a leaf. Most of the time he is alone, and his solitude causes him pain, particularly in a society which values a superficial togetherness. And when life is through with him, it simply blows him away or, if he is lucky, permits him to wither and drop. These thoughts and emotions are surely part of Cummings' poem, but by no means all of it.

As we have seen, Cummings' leaf does not merely plummet meaninglessly to earth. It also slips and twists with the grace and delicacy and symmetry of circus acrobats. In his play *Him*, written in 1927, Cummings' artist-hero refers specifically to the circus in a climactic moment of self-discovery. Acrobats, because they perform in the face of death, are completely and exhilaratingly and uniquely aware of themselves. "The average 'painter' 'sculptor' 'poet' 'composer' 'playwright' is a person who cannot leap through a hoop from the back of a galloping horse, make people laugh with a clown's mouth, orchestrate twenty lions," he says. "But imagine a human being who balances three chairs, one on top of another, on a wire, eighty feet in air with no net underneath, and then climbs into the top chair, sits down, and begins to swing. . . ."

The leaf falling is like this acrobat, and it also is like the bullfighters that Cummings' contemporary, Ernest Hemingway, wrote about. According to Hemingway, the test of a bullfighter was his ability to perform graceful movements close to the bull's horns. Good bullfighters provided living symbols of man's ability to live with dignity, despite the everpresent threat of dissolution. Indeed, by implication, the sharper his awareness of death, the greater his dignity. The particular quality of experience that

Cummings invites us to share is also very like the one which the Bible cites in enjoining us, "He who would find himself, must lose himself." Athletes know an approximation of this ideal in the moment when, after long hours of practice, they suddenly find that they do not have to think about what they are doing. They don't have to struggle to avoid particular errors; they can just relax and let their muscles take over. They reach their highest perfection in a unique kind of awareness which is self-forgetting.

Ultimately, this self-forgetting is what Cummings' treatment of "loneliness" adds up to also. We have seen how "iness" resolves the sounds, the action, and the word "loneliness" itself. But the line resolves a dimension of meaning as well. Dividing the word "loneliness" has produced an insistent emphasis on the idea of oneness. It is as though Cummings had shown us that the inner meaning of man's unhappy isolation is his very preoccupation with himself. Significantly, then, at the end, he also gives us an image of the ultimate nature of human being: lower-case "i-ness." The poem which ends in a sense of serenity, of unhappiness and death somehow resolved, explains itself ultimately in terms of that special self-forgetting which is utter humility. The movement of the poem has not been swift and rollicking, full of confidence in the possibility of human transcendence. It has, instead, been slow, difficult, even severe, suggesting the hard-won, disciplined achievement of a tragic self-knowledge.[2]

II "nonsun blob"

In 1954 William Carlos Williams, a friend of Cummings' and a fine poet in his own right, wrote an article about Cummings' poems and paintings.[3] He cited the opening poem from Cummings' 1944 volume, one times one, and said: he who understands these lines understands E. E. Cummings. Williams' is a difficult test, for the poem demands more of its readers than almost any other in the Cummings canon; and yet it is, as Williams implied, a small masterpiece. The poem follows:

> nonsun blob a
> cold to
> skylessness
> sticking fire

> my are your
> are birds our all
> and one gone
> away the they
>
> leaf of ghosts some
> few creep there
> here or on
> unearth

The poem pricks and challenges. It begins with a line that is
almost nonsense. Far from being a syntactical unit, the first
stanza contains nothing even faintly like a verb. The second
stanza is, if possible, more frustrating yet. It seems to assert
something but is, at the very least, so elliptical as to be gibberish.
The poem is not a picture of anything. It is not even composed,
as the "loneliness" poem is, of recognizable linguistic units which
have simply been broken up and rearranged. To approach this
poem as though it involved some solvable trick of syntactic
dislocation is to miss its revolutionary nature.[4] No poem quite
like it was ever written before.

If we would read it, we must put aside our preconceptions,
open our pores, flex our wits, and, paraphrasing Williams, do
precisely what Cummings wants us to do. Each stanza, each
line, each word demands separate exploration in relation to the
others. The quality of mind that the poem demands is the fresh
and innocent one which, as it were, must search the world and
decide anew whether the object lying at its feet should be called
"not-me," quadruped, black and white thing, cocker spaniel, or
my dog Fido. It must seek significant relationships. To do so, it
must return to the simplest of mental operations and ask:
"Which things seem to belong together and which are opposed?"
In some sense, most art demands this elemental sort of response.
What is unique about Cummings' poem, as with much of
twentieth-century art, is that it yields all or nothing.

Whatever it may mean, the fourth line "sticking fire" is a
sharp contrast to the cold, shapeless notquiteanything which
Cummings insists upon in the first three lines. It has color; it
has shape; it is hot. When we make our first discovery about
the poem, we realize that something has happened in the first
stanza. Lacking the clues of logic, we have difficulty locating

ourselves in Cummings' astronomy. The event might be the birth
of the universe, the earth's bursting into spring, or day-break.
Williams suggested that the poem was about Cummings' intoxi-
cation with women and noted that Cummings is "a veritable
Puritan with his pornography whenever he is forced to use it."
This view suggests that "sticking fire" symbolizes the birth of
sexual love. But a traumatic beginning, certainly!

The second stanza continues the growth which began in the
first. Apart from their meaning, the words of the first two lines
("my are your/are birds our all") form two mathematical equa-
tions. One says, "my + your = our." The other, based on the
phonetic pun, "our" and "are," says, "my = your"; "my + your
= birds"; "my + your + birds = all." Translated into a lesser
language, the lines say that the world is one. But what Cummings has done is to stage before our eyes the process of growth
by which that which was born in the first stanza gradually
expands into a soaring, all-encompassing unity. And the clear
implication of the possessive pronouns, which merge mine into
yours into ours into all, is that the nature of the unity is love.
In the almost incredibly circumscribed space of seven words,
Cummings dramatizes the process which Dostoevsky describes
in a paragraph in *The Brothers Karamazov*:

> Love a man even in his sin, for that is the semblance of
> Divine Love and is the highest love on earth. Love all
> God's creation, the whole and every grain of sand in it.
> Love the animals, love the plants, love everything. If you
> love everything, you will perceive the divine mystery in
> things. Once you perceive it, you will begin to compre-
> hend it better every day. And you will come at last to love
> the whole world with an all-embracing love.

Cummings does not argue or instruct. He directs us as though we
were actors in a play. In the middle of the third act we have
come to recognize what it feels like to participate in a process
of creation and growth to fulfillment.

From the middle of the poem to the end, all is declining
action. Cummings picks up the bird image, which he has used
partly to represent the animal kingdom and partly to suggest
the exalted feeling of soaring flight, and depicts a flock of birds
suddenly pursuing a departed leader. The created unity dis-

solves rapidly. The sense of a world of "we" dissipates into I and "they." The last stanza completes the circle. For a moment after the birds depart, some ghostly vestiges remain visible. The image of the leaf suggests an autumnal scene but, significantly, confirms also that the vegetable kingdom was part of the perfect "all." Finally, the progress from "there" to "here" to "unearth" suggests the declining light of day. In the enveloping darkness the eye can see into the distance, then only what is nearby, and, at the end, nothing at all.

The progress of the poem has been from nothing to nothing, from birth to death. Like the author of *Revelation,* the reader has seen a vision of the Alpha and the Omega, the first and the last, the beginning and the end. The struggle to discard conventional expectations in order to read Cummings' poem has been long, yet the poem is short, and the total experience of the poem is short. That is, our sense of the poem is of something exquisitely shaped but also extremely small. We have been led to witness a lifetime collapsed into a moment. Is this the total import of the poem? Is the poem finally a comment on the evanescence of life? Are we left to sip a cup of gall in the knowledge that whatever joy or beauty or achievement we have in our life is soon to disappear? To some extent, the answer must certainly be, yes. But, just like "loneliness," this poem is not mere gall.

One of the pivotal words is the "and" that begins the poem's second half. Not even poets, whose business is condensation, ordinarily require such commonplace words as "and" to work as hard as Cummings requires this one to. But in a poem of only thirty-two words, every stroke must contribute. "And" serves here particularly to energize a tonal development which would otherwise have begun to flag along with the disintegration which is the rest of the poem. It is startling to realize the significance of Cummings' choice of "and." If we stop to think a moment, the expected word is "but"! We would expect Cummings to say, "I had a vision of birth and growth and of the purest, most magnificent harmony, *but* it all fell apart, died, and disappeared." The effect of Cummings' "and" is to sustain a quality of expectant wonder, for the "and" implies that the development in the poem is not only ascent and descent but also one continuous process of growth.

If we look closely at the third stanza to ascertain what kind of growth Cummings has offered us, we find significant suggestions of a spiritual development. The ghosts may be vestiges of the middle of the poem's unified "all," but they are at the same time creeping souls or spirits in the process of becoming a new quality of *unearthliness,* and the nighttime-death which shuts off vision of the physical world opens up at the same time a vision of the mysterious world of spirit. Readers who thought William Carlos Williams' sexual interpretation of the poem somewhat far-fetched may now regard it more sympathetically, having discovered in the poem the experience of a physical death which is also a spiritual reawakening. Williams' reading recalls an illuminating passage written by a well-known Dutch gynecologist concerning the last stages of coitus:

> And the most profound and exquisite happiness which human beings can taste, is tasted by couples who truly *love* one another, during this pause of respite and realisation, after completed communion. Far, far more closely than even the rapture of mutual orgasm does this bliss and content of the *after-glow* unite true lovers, as they lie embraced, side by side, while nature recuperates, and their thoughts, in a waking dream, once more live through the joys they have experienced, and their souls meet and merge, even though their bodies are no longer linked.[5]

Whether or not Cummings' poem is about the love of a man and woman, it is certainly very like it, particularly in the way a climax leads simultaneously to a physical dissipation and to a psychological and spiritual fulfillment.

If Cummings' handling of diction and syntax is unconventional, he uses sound patterns skillfully and subtly and conventionally. Indeed, we who cannot make our way through the poem may find our first insights into the development of its tone and its meaning through its music. The effect of nothingness, of nonsense and negation in the first line, for example, gets an important assist from its metrical arrangement. If the line had been reversed, that is, set down in the normal pattern of English syntax—article, adjective, noun—the result would have been a commonplace iambic dimeter meter:

Four Poems

$$x \quad / \quad x \quad /$$
a nonsun blob

As Cummings wrote it, it has four accented syllables.

$$/ \quad / \quad / \quad /$$
nonsun blob a

The result is a line without emphasis, difficult to read, distinct in its undistinction. The following two lines soften the opening harshness with one and two unaccented syllables respectively and prepare for the shocking fourth line. The elongation of line three with its two successive unaccented syllables gives the accented opening of "sticking fire" a special thrust. Cummings might have written "cold to/darkness." But line four gains the force of contrast from the extra syllable of "skylessness" and also from the assonance of "sky" and "fire."

Stanza two is a fine piece of sound organization just as it is of condensed meaning. The first two lines are unified by their multiplicity of "r" sounds and short vowels. More important, they establish clearly the iambic center toward which the poem has been moving. "My are your" is metrically identical to "sticking fire," but the climactic "are birds our all" is a satisfyingly regular, two iambic feet. The abrupt departure of the first bird is accented by the short three-syllable line, by the internal eye-rhyme of "one" and "gone," and by the sharp juxtaposition of two accented syllables. By contrast the graceful flight of the rest of the birds is paralleled in the sound of a full rhyme and in the return to a rhythmically regular iambic dimeter in "away the they."

The last stanza begins irregularly. The second line, in particular, is composed of three accented syllables. From this irregularity the third line serves as a brilliant transition to the finale. Metrically, "here or on" repeats the earlier transition, "my are your." In addition, however, the difficulty of enunciating a line without any hard consonants (contrast the relative ease of saying, "here to be") slows the pace leading to the pungently short and satisfyingly regular, iambic "unearth." Cummings has used well the resources of versification traditionally available to English language poets, and his final return to iambic meter is at least as persuasive a means of communicating his feeling as his development of imagery. The last line is in every way Cummings' serene affirmation that an end is also a beginning.

Beyond noting their oddity and their relationship to versification, we have so far paid little heed to Cummings' diction and syntax. Once again, however, a search for surface pattern reveals inner meaning, for a close inspection of the poet's words and of their arrangement yields the growth of a human mind. In every respect the first line is a kind of sub-baby talk. Its inversion of normal word order, its utter vagueness, its emphasis on each syllable equally—all suggest the most rudimentary quality of mind. Taken by itself, it is nonsense and sounds like nothing so much as a small child painfully reading words he does not understand. The first stanza as a whole is not much different.

As noted earlier, the beginning of the second stanza includes verbs and, in asserting identities, primitively establishes relationships. Suddenly, however, in the last two lines of stanza two, the poem presents a markedly clear syntactical relationship, and a sophisticated one at that. The lines "and one gone/away the they," even without punctuation, involve a clear logical subordination. They say, "After (or perhaps, because) one had gone, the others went away."

The third stanza is syntactically the most highly organized and sophisticated in the poem. The subject is somewhat obscure and the word order is a little scrambled; otherwise, it is a perfectly conventional English sentence: "Some few ghosts of leaf creep there, here, or on unearth."

Similar growth informs the poem's diction. The clearest illustration is the development from "a" to "the" to "some few." The dictionary says of the indefinite article: "A connotes a thing not previously noted or recognized, in contrast with *the*, which connotes a thing previously noted or recognized." The mind of the poem has, therefore, grown when it develops the capacity to remember previous experience and to compare it to the present. But the ability to say "some few" represents an even more complex, mental operation, for it involves distinguishing the category of ghosts from other aspects of past experience, but also recognizing that a small number only of the whole category is present.

The poem, which we have previously talked about as the history of a universe, a year, a day, a sexual experience, and a human soul, is also then the history of a human mind. Like the soul, but unlike the other "subjects" of the poem, the mind develops in a straight line rather than in a rising and falling action. It differs from all the other subjects, however, in that it never reaches full development. It never achieves the ability to conceptualize fully its experience, and this incomplete growth is also part of the poem's meaning. In the first place, it adds a kind of wispiness to the ending which is otherwise fully rounded, complete, and symmetrical. It is a highly appropriate quality for the launching of a soul into mysterious, otherworldly waters. We may even speculate that the completely formed intellect would be unfit for such a launching. The intellectual, Cummings may be saying, has, like the rich man, as much chance of getting into the kingdom of heaven as a camel through the eye of a needle. This speculation gains peculiar force when we consider how profound an assault on rationality the whole poem has been. Cummings has forced the reader to feel his language, to listen to his music, and to study his pictures; he has done everything possible to bypass the intellect, for thus only could he get us to enter experientially into the meaning of his poem. In other poems Cummings insists that the intellect separates man from full, vitalizing knowledge even of the physical world; and it may be significant that, in this poem, the intellect is gaining its greatest strength at the end of the birth-death cycle when little remains to be seen and understood. The intellect is not wholly to be denied, but it must somehow work cooperatively with the innocence of a child, with the senses, the emotions, the soul. It must work esthetically.

III "*Among these red pieces of day*"

Not all of Cummings' poems present imposing difficulties even on a first reading. The surface of the following poem is troubled neither by words-within-words nor by strikingly unusual syntax or diction. It is unconventional but easily readable. The danger in reading this poem is that we may pass over it too quickly, for, like many of Cummings' poems, it has a quality of super-realism. A simple, direct presentation of a miniature narrative, it communicates with such precision that, if inattentive, we may fail to see how far its meaning extends beyond itself.

Among

these
red pieces of
day(against which and
quite silently hills
made of blueandgreen paper

scorchbend ingthem
-selves-U
pcurv E,into:
anguish(clim
b)ing
s-p-i-r-a-
l
 and,disappear)
Satanic and blasé
a black goat lookingly wanders

There is nothing left of the world but
into this noth
ing il treno per
Roma si-gnori?
jerk.
ilyr,ushes

[*Poems 1923-1954*, pp. 199-200]

A man looks up into the hills at sunset and sees a goat; a train conductor announces the train for Rome; the train leaves. Nothing very exciting seems to have happened. The traveler in his entranced observation of the hills may narrowly have avoided missing his train, but the poem is certainly not Hollywood melodrama. It has none of the qualities of the perils of Pauline. Nor does the poem seem to invoke any of the attitudes we normally associate with beautifully red sunsets. There is no explicit comment about the glory of God's universe, and nothing about the peace and serenity of evening. Yet the poem has an air of importance, as though something meaningful had occurred, something which is at once too deep and too fleeting for clear articulation.

The opening lines are highly abstract. We cannot visualize

"pieces of day," even red ones. We cannot even be sure, at this stage of the poem, that the poet is talking about evening rather than dawn. But, whatever it means, "pieces" suggests the traveler's sense of the day as smashed or being smashed—not pure and still but shattered like broken crockery. In addition, the spacing of the opening lines gives each word, especially the first two, unusual weight and emphasis, as though the traveler were beginning some sort of struggle, perhaps trying to focus his attention on the scene before him or searching for the right words with which to characterize its special qualities.

The parenthetical representation of the hills is acutely observed: "against which" stresses the relationship of the "blueandgreen" hills to the "red" sky, and because of this stress the hills seem to be ascending rather than the sun descending. The effect is to suggest the intentness with which the traveler is looking up at the hills. In addition, Cummings has used a variety of his own inventions to render the precise qualities of the hills in the setting sun. Special punctuation, varying line length, and word fragmentation emphasize their generally slow, heavy but uneven progress. The splitting of "upcurve" into three parts gives the word extreme weight, suggesting laborious effort. At the same time the isolated letter "U" and the presence of capital letters at both the beginning and the end of the word emphasize the magnitude of the action by demonstrating visually the very meaning of "upcurve." The simple comma and the small, unfragmented, quickly enunciated word "into," which follow, provide a moment's respite, but the colon emphasizes that it is merely a moment and that more, weighty action is to come. The fragmenting of "climb" (as well as its denotative meaning) likewise demands heavy emphasis, and the hyphens in "spiral" are especially insistent. The final "l," on the other hand, suggests visually the hills' last upward motion, thereby preparing for the last line of the parenthesis, "and,disappear," a line which, by contrast to the preceding lines, reads simply and rapidly.

In general, the strangeness of these lines is Cummings' effort to indicate the precise timing with which they are to be read, and the timing forces us into a muscular identification with the action itself. Not all the poet's directions can be followed vocally. Although a word like "climb" should receive vocal stress, Cummings does not intend that we make any special effort to enunciate the separated, final "b." The full impact depends on a visual communication to the "inner ear." The voice holds the long "i," but the inner ear adds the visual effort of searching from one line to the next in order to find the end of the word.

The traveler's total impression of the sky and hills in the twilight hours is of a great bonfire. The hills, like burning paper, twist and curl upward and finally disappear into night. They are fragile and delicate, and their final disappearance is rapid and total; yet at the same time their destruction is a gigantic action. The traveler witnesses with fascinated horror the earth's final death agony, as it were, in one last, great conflagration.

When the opening sentence finally reaches its destination ("a black goat lookingly wanders"), its brevity and the ease with which it can be read contain an important part of its meaning. The disproportionate time and effort required to read the two parts of the sentence parallel the disproportion between the size and importance of the scene of destruction and the goat's utter indifference. The contrast is sharpened by the color contrasts (red—blueandgreen—black), and Cummings' invention of the adverb "lookingly" effectively italicizes the vacancy of the goat's stare. The anti-climactic quality of the sentence reflects, in short, the traveler's sense of stunned horror in realizing that the goat neither sees nor cares what is going on around him. His "Satanism" lies precisely in this insensitivity. Life has moved irrevocably toward destruction, and the goat is aware of neither the lost world nor the traveler. The effect on the traveler is to magnify his own sense of loss, even dispossession.

Although by no means a necessary part of the poem, the poem is nevertheless enriched if we remember Jesus' use of goats as an image of the damned in a prophetic description of Judgment Day. According to Matthew 25:31-46, Jesus said that all the nations would be separated "as a shepherd separates the sheep from the goats." The goats are damned because, like Cummings' goat, they are unresponsive to the world. They are incapable of perceiving and sharing the sufferings of others. This allusion involves a major irony, however, for in the biblical account of the last day it is the goats who are dispatched to "the eternal fire prepared for the devil and his angels." In Cummings' poem, the goat is oblivious to the fire; it is the intensely responsive traveler who stares, awe-struck, at the fire's destructive power.

This irony is peculiarly appropriate, however, as the final section of the poem reveals. Technically speaking, the last section establishes the dramatic situation. That is, we discover only at the end of the poem that the speaker is a traveler standing in a European railway station. Dramatically speaking, however, the last section renders the traveler's sense of a sudden, momentous return of life. The traveler has no sooner expressed his ultimately lonely and fateful sense of having lost the world ("There is nothing left of the world") than the most ordinary train announcement breaks into his consciousness with all the sharpness of a thunderclap. The traveler suddenly realizes that he is himself a goat. He has been standing on a crowded station platform (the plural form of the Italian word for "Sir" indicates that he was, at least, not alone), totally oblivious to the sights and sounds immediately around him, totally preoccupied by the constructions of his own mind. In his fascination with the morbid implications of distant things, he has been unresponsive to the actuality of the close-at-hand.

The foreign language underscores, to be sure, the traveler's sense of alienation, but the pure sound of the conductor's voice, entering as it does disembodied and without warning, as though from another world, renders implicitly how alert and sensitive the traveler has suddenly become to his surroundings. Finally, the poem renders another, even lesser sense experience, the initial lurch, gathering momentum, and slightly delayed-action take-off of the departing train. Feeling the motion of the train has become, in the total context of the poem, peculiarly important; for in his ability to respond to the most immediate and ordinary of sense experiences, quite apart from their philosophical or practical meaning, the traveler has made a new beginning in life. His loneliness remains, but the world, no longer a mere "nothing," has acquired new value.

We must be careful not to overstate the significance either of the poem or of the incident which it represents. The poem is relaxed and informal, not tightly knit like "nonsun blob." The description of the rising hills is flawed by the word "anguish," which too insistently labels the meaning of the action. No particular advantage is gained by hyphenating "si-gnori." The incident itself is neither complex nor profound. Becoming lost in thought and suddenly having the world intrude is a common experience of all men, and that really is all the poem is about. But the poem is concrete, precisely sensed, and rigorously selective in its detail. It takes the special alertness and skill of a poet to see in such an ordinary, apparently insignificant moment, a metaphor of life itself, and then to manage the reconstruction of the moment so that we can see and, in seeing, realize that we too are, for the most part, goats, sinfully preoccupied with our own hopes and fears, blind to the sensuous reality of the given world.[6]

IV *"anyone lived in a pretty how town"*

The poem which follows, "anyone lived in a pretty how town," bears several interesting relationships to the poems already discussed. More than any of them it *looks* like a poem. It is organized into a series of quatrains and, despite irregularities, into rhyme and meter. It is a narrative like "Among these red pieces of day." Like "nonsun blob," it collapses a long time span into a short space. Also like "nonsun blob," it is abstract rather than concretely realistic. Like all three previous poems, but perhaps more clearly than any of them, it presents Cummings' whole metaphysic. Unlike any of the others, "anyone lived in a pretty how town" is one of Cummings' best known, most generally admired poems. The others deserve to be better known; this one deserves the reputation it has.

> anyone lived in a pretty how town
> (with up so floating many bells down)
> spring summer autumn winter
> he sang his didn't he danced his did
>
> Women and men(both little and small)
> cared for anyone not at all
> they sowed their isn't they reaped their same
> sun moon stars rain
>
> children guessed(but only a few
> and down they forgot as up they grew
> autumn winter spring summer)
> that noone loved him more by more

> when by now and tree by leaf
> she laughed his joy she cried his grief
> bird by snow and stir by still
> anyone's any was all to her
>
> someones married their everyones
> laughed their cryings and did their dance
> (sleep wake hope and then) they
> said their nevers they slept their dream
>
> stars rain sun moon
> (and only the snow can begin to explain
> how children are apt to forget to remember
> with up so floating many bells down)
>
> one day anyone died i guess
> (and noone stooped to kiss his face)
> busy folk buried them side by side
> little by little and was by was
>
> all by all and deep by deep
> and more by more they dream their sleep
> noone and anyone earth by april
> wish by spirit and if by yes
>
> Women and men (both dong and ding)
> summer autumn winter spring
> reaped their sowing and went their came
> sun moon stars rain
>
> [*Poems 1923-1954*, pp. 370-1]

The narrative is very simple. Anyone and noone are lovers. Cummings does not say whether they ever marry. What is important is that they love life and each other. They die, and in dying, they merge their love with the love at the heart of things. Bells ring. Day turns to night and back to day again. The weather changes. The seasons revolve. Children become adults. And that is the story.

The primary interest is the firm and sometimes subtle series of contrasts which define the two leading characters, the other adults in the town, and the children. The structure of the poem underlines these contrasts. It consists of three sections, in each of which (except the last) one stanza treats anyone and noone, one treats the "Women and men," and one, the children. This structure of contrasts is paralleled by the characters' very names.

The opening line of the poem is somewhat puzzling until we learn in line four that "anyone" is not an indefinite but a particular person. The next stanza squares this initial ambiguity. In observing that the adults of the town "cared for anyone not at all," Cummings says both that they do not care for the hero of the poem and that they do not care for anybody at all. But, in addition, he says that the townsfolk are the indefinite ones, indistinguishable from one another. The differences among them range only from "little" to "small." Paradoxically, they are the ones who really deserve to be called "anyones"; "anyone," on the other hand, is not only a particular person but a very particular person. He is indeed the complete individualist. The ultimate significance of the names in the poem, therefore, lies in the double contrast they make about the characters' spiritual as well as social values. "Anyone" and "noone" are individualists, whole persons because they have no pride. They do not strive to make names for themselves. In their spiritual humility and their willingness therefore to be, socially, just anyone, they are capable of love. The townsfolk, on the other hand, are status conscious. They make judgments, to use the language of both the poem and American colloquial speech, about who is a somebody and who is a nobody. Each of them wants very much to make something of himself and to be somebody. They are concerned about what "everyone" is saying, doing, and thinking. They tend to be empty conformists because, in their preoccupation with conventional measures of behavior and human worth, they have lost their souls.

These contrasts are implicit in the characters' names; they are fully developed in the characters' relations with the world, with their work and play, the round of nature, death, religion. "Anyone," for example, "sang his didn't he danced his did." This mysteriously communicative line suggests that "anyone" responded joyfully not only to periods of work and relaxation but to failure as well as success. Because he did not expect life to be his constant servant, he accepted the world as it was given to him. He lived as though he had heard and believed the famous passage in the Sermon on the Mount which says, "Look at the birds of the air: they neither sow nor reap nor gather into barns, and yet your heavenly Father feeds them. Are you not of more value than they?" "Someones," on the other hand, faithlessly and therefore anxiously, "sowed their isn't they reaped their same." And their anxiety colors their play as well as their work; for, whereas "anyone" "danced his did," "someones" and "everyones" "did their dance." The suggestion is that they danced dutifully, without humor or joy or even much pleasure.

Because "anyone" and "noone" glide with the current, even death is a creative event. They are able to grow and finally blossom. They have lived fully when alive; in death they become "was by was," and the ultimate sleep is, for them, ultimate fulfillment. They move into the present tense ("they *dream* their sleep") as nobody else in the poem ever does. Their development parallels the natural progress of day and night, the weather and the seasons. "Someones" and "everyones," on the other hand, hold life at bay. Their religion is a series of "nevers." And one of the subtle implications of the poem is that, because they are not really alive, they are incapable of dying. Because they are "isn't," they are incapable of becoming "was by was." They remain forever in the past tense. They do not grow naturally; they do not even change. For them, significantly, the poem closes as it opened. The line which says that they "reaped their sowing and went their came" is a direct echo of the early line, "they sowed their isn't they reaped their same." Despite the majestic round of the earth, implicit in the four-stress line "sun moon stars rain," and despite their opportunity to learn from the example of "anyone" and "noone," their lives are as empty and meaningless as the mechanical "dong and ding" of the clock which rules their coming and going, their eating and sleeping, their work and "play."

The really pathetic people in the poem, however, are not the townspeople but their children. In an indirect but far more significant way than "anyone" and "noone," they die onstage. Indeed, in an important sense, their death is the center of the poem. As stanza three indicates, the children had the sensitivity to recognize "anyone" and "noone's" love, and a few actually did. But when they grew up (that is, grew older), they lost their special sensitivity, and those that had known love forgot it. They lost, that is, their capacity to live and became "isn't" like the other townsfolk. In stanza six Cummings returns to the children to comment that their spiritual death is an utter mystery. The structure of the poem leads us to expect some reference to the children again in stanza nine; and, when this expectation is frustrated, we realize that such a reference would be entirely inappropriate. The children no longer exist. They have passed on—into adulthood. And we realize further that the bells have been ringing their passage.

The bells appear in the poem four times. The second line, "(with up so floating many bells down)," by its very rhythm, suggests the swinging of great church bells. It introduces the bells as a major motif of the poem and, through close juxta-position, implies that they are the outstanding characteristic of the town. The bells are actually heard on only two other occa-sions—in the stanzas which present and comment on the death of the children. In stanza three the bells literally announce their death: "and down they forgot as up they grew." In stanza six the original sounds are repeated exactly, ("with up so floating many bells down"), as though, when Cummings thinks about the children, he can hear their funeral in the background. Finally, the last stanza, while omitting the expected reference to children, indicates what has happened to them in its parenthetical asser-tion that the town's adults are symbolically identical to the bells: "Women and men(both dong and ding)." In contrast to "anyone" and "noone" who have passed through death into new life, the children have passed through new life into death. In contrast to the natural growth of "anyone" and "noone," the children have entered the merely mechanical existence, sym-bolized by the endless swing back and forth of the town's bells.

It remains to ask how Cummings feels about the characters and the action represented in his poem. When a man speaks, his meaning depends heavily on his tone of voice. Does Cum-mings' tone indicate that he is sad, angry, sarcastic? How does he evaluate "anyone's" and "someones'" "pretty how town" and the larger world in which it exists?

In other poems Cummings was utterly contemptuous of the pride which enslaves men to an anxious search for security and status and happiness. Exercising his sharpest sarcasm, he once referred to man as "this fine specimen of hypermagical ultra-omnipotence." This contempt is, implicitly, Cummings' attitude

toward the "busy folk" in "anyone lived in a pretty how town."
And yet the tone of the poem does not divide neatly to match
the basic contrast between the two lovers and the town. Cummings is neither wholly lyrical about "anyone" and "noone" nor
wholly contemptuous about "someones" and "everyones." To be
sure, he shows favoritism. The four lines in the poem which
deal specifically with the relationship between "anyone" and
"noone" are the only four completely regular iambic lines in an
otherwise metrically irregular poem. The lines are:

```
    x  /  x  /  x  /  x  /
    that noone loved him more by more
    x  /  x  /  x  /  x  /
    she laughed his joy she cried his grief
    x  /  x  /  x  /  x  /
    (and noone stooped to kiss his face
    x  /  x  /  x  /  x  /
    and more by more they dream their sleep
```

This use of meter comments on the nature of "normality" in
Cummings' conception of things. But, generally speaking, Cummings plays out the role he values. His attitude toward the
characters and the action of his story is like "anyone's" when
"he sang his didn't he danced his did." Despite the pathos of
the children's demise, the triumph of "anyone's" and "noone's"
rebirth, and the horror of the townspeople's continuing hollowness, Cummings maintains his composure. He sings of victory;
he dances defeat. In the very manner in which he tells his story
he gaily turns sense into nonsense and nonsense into sense. He
makes abstractions concrete—most obviously in the case of the
words "anyone" and "noone." He takes colloquial expressions
with specific meanings, removes the meanings, and plays with
their formal properties. He starts, for example, in stanza seven
with the conventional expression "side by side." He adds to it
another expression "little by little," except that he discards its
conventional meaning ("gradually"): he means, literally, two
little people lying next to one another. Using the same structural
formula he continues to add phrases which become increasingly
untranslatable and yet somehow appropriate. The phrase "more
by more" echoes the colloquial "more and more," as it did earlier
in the poem; but Cummings has turned the simple addition of the

conventional expression into multiplication in order to express the depth of "anyone's" and "noone's" union. By the time the series reaches the lines:

> noone and anyone earth by april
> wish by spirit and if by yes

the combination of denotation, rhythm, and sound is so subtle as to be a species of magic. The only way to gain perspective on Cummings' achievement is to rewrite the lines and inspect the contrast. Here, for example, is a revision which keeps Cummings' syntax and rhythm:

> noone and anyone mud by iron
> hope by never and since by no

Their inappropriateness by contrast to Cummings' lines is either self-evident or the reader is immune to magic. Every good poem has a limit beyond which analysis is helpless. That limit is unusually close in the case of these lines from "anyone lived in a pretty how town." Their special charm has, moreover, a peculiar fitness to the poem's total context because, in the largest sense, it is what the poem is about. "Anyone" and "noone" have attuned their lives to something very like the magical charm of these lines.

In his role as poet, therefore, Cummings acts out the meaning of his poem. He takes obvious pleasure in imitating the sound of the bells despite their symbolic meaning. He is casually playful about the children's pitiful maturation, as the following lines clearly suggest:

> (and only the snow can begin to explain
> how children are apt to forget to remember

The only time he intrudes directly upon the narrative, ("one day anyone died i guess"), the intrusion emphasizes the unimportance of "anyone's" death, which might otherwise be regarded as a critical turning point in the story. The poet suggests, by using an uncapitalized "i," that his strangely detached attitude reflects his own sense of the unimportance of self, mankind, and physical life and the overriding importance of love, the soul, and the transcendent life of God's creation.

[44]

Four Poems

The success of "anyone lived in a pretty how town" lies in its complex wholeness. It is angry, sad, joyous. It is realistic about the possibility of improving the average man and yet prophetic concerning the ultimate reality of love. But narrative action, characterization, tone, theme, and language are all tightly interwoven. Together they create an effect of unconventional but convincing simplicity; and, at last, this simplicity may be the poem's central meaning. The magical simplicity of life itself, it says, is the reason for living.[7]

CHAPTER 2

For of Such Is the Kingdom

"I thank You God for. . . everything which is natural which is
infinite which is yes"

I *Immediacy*

SOME OF Cummings' best known and most delightful verse
bounces and skips like a child. It plays the way a child
plays, and it cuts through to the essence of things as only a
child can. It asks questions about matters which adults have
long taken for granted or are too polite to mention. It exults
in experiences which grown-ups have forgotten. It shouts and
laughs and sings and dances with wild abandon. Cummings'
first volume of poems, *Tulips and Chimneys* (1923), included a
short section entitled, "Chansons Innocentes" (after Blake's *Songs
of Innocence*). The first poem remains a best-beloved one both of
Cummings' admirers and of the poet himself, who frequently
selected it for public performances and read it with obvious
pleasure.

> in Just-
> spring   when the world is mud-
> luscious the little
> lame balloonman
>
> whistles   far   and wee
>
> and eddieandbill come
> running from marbles and
> piracies and it's
> spring

          when the world is puddle-wonderful

          the queer
          old ballooonman whistles
          far   and   wee
          and bettyandisbel come dancing

          from hop-scotch and jump-rope and

          it's
          spring
          and
                   the

                   goat-footed

          balloonMan   whistles
          far
          and
          wee

                        [*Poems 1923-1954*, pp. 21-22]

Quite remarkable in its simplicity, "in Just-spring" witnesses the
baptismal quality of spring when the world is born anew and
men feel a quickened sense of spontaneous joy. The speaker
watches boys and girls at play on a city street or playground.
The spacing of his words suggests the children's shared pleasure,
the instinctive hurry and jostle of their play, and their delight
in the balloonman's appearance. But the speaker does more
than watch. He too shares the spring feeling. He gaily invents
words, like "mud-luscious" and "puddle-wonderful," which in
both sound and meaning signify his intuitive response to the
children's play. His words rush out, somewhat incoherently but
with emphatic repetition. As the children might themselves, he
drops in his hurry a syllable from the name Isabel. The balloon
man is, to him, not a man who sells balloons but a "balloonman."

   His patient attention to the progress of the balloonman as he
moves into sight and then out again is more adult than childlike,
but it is likely the children's interest which directed his vision
in the first place. Their response to spring and to each other is
undoubtedly responsible for the speaker's imagining, as the
balloonman disappears into the pure spring air, that the goat-
footed god Pan himself has blessed the scene.

Cummings continued to value the child's capacity to see vividly and to respond freshly and immediately down to his last
volume of poems. Throughout his writing career, psychologists
and sociologists studied the process of human perception. They
found increasingly accurate means of demonstrating the principle that people do not first see and then know; rather, they
first know and then see. In the Boston schools, for example, an
experiment showed that poor pupils consistently overestimated
(while wealthy pupils underestimated) the physical size of coins.
As Cummings understood them, children see, hear, and smell
with precision and accuracy until they are led out of themselves—that is to say, educated—into adulthood. Then they perceive what everyone else perceives, as adults have taught
them.

But children are the true "teachers." If adults will pay attention, children can teach them truly to see again. Like the observer
of "eddieandbill," the father in #43 of *95 Poems* feels a quickened sense of life's meaning as he and his child look out a
window together and watch the snow fall. Eyes by eyes they
stare. And the white sky and white air soon make a white earth:

eyes eyes

looking (alw
ays) while
earth and sky grow
one with won

der. . .

As the parenthetical "always" suggests in this section from the
poem, they are simultaneously all "eyes," all I's, and all yesses.
They do not think about the meaning of winter, not even about
such "poetic" meanings as the winter of old age and death; they
do not think about the economics of snow-removal; nor even
about what they might be doing if it were not snowing. They
look at the snow. They watch it fall with wonder and delight;
and, as the poem develops, father and son give themselves up
to the scene and, in the process, share an experience in which
they sense the ultimate victory of unity over fragmentation.
They feel the oneness not only of earth and sky but of them-

selves. They experience, that is, not what they are supposed to, but what, in E. E. Cummings' world, is really there.

Cummings' strategy in using children in his poetry is most apparent, however, in those poems in which children and adults clash. The directness of young, untutored perceptions reveals by contrast the sterility and, finally, the very immorality of much of adult life in America. Children, unmarred by ideas, are, as Cummings once said, "uncouthly alive." The opening poem in the volume *Viva*, for example, while not particularly successful poetry, nevertheless illuminatingly dramatizes the experiences during one evening and one morning of children and adults who live in an apartment hotel.[1] Presented as it impinges upon the child's mind, the action includes the children struggling into their night-clothes, the nighttime noises from adult living rooms and the world outside, a morning elevator ride, and a walk on a city street. The poem is about uncouth aliveness and couth deadness:

,mean-
hum
a)now

(nit
y unb
uria

ble fore(hurry
into
heads are
legs think wrists

argue)short(eyes do
bang hands angle
scoot bulbs marry a become)
ened
(to is

see!so
long door
golf slam bridge train shriek
chewing whistles hugest
to
morrow from smiles sin

k
ingly ele
vator glide pinn
)pu(
acle to

rubber)tres(plants how grin
ho)cen(tel
und
ead the

not stroll
living spawn imitate)ce(re
peat

credo fais do
do neighbors re babies
                                while;

The core of the adult world revealed in this poem is a hollow, purposeless, madly rushing self-preoccupation. The adults hurry their children into their pajamas, hurriedly shut the lights off, and hurriedly say, "so long." The rush is all about a bridge game with the neighbors. They rush downstairs by elevator and rush through a morning "stroll." They rush in order to : . . . Whatever the goal, it's always in the future, never now. They never quite manage to be alive, because they are always planning their time, hurrying to keep up to the schedule, because, if they do, life will be—tomorrow. Adults foreshorten present time with plans for the future just as, in the poem, "now" is buried under parenthetical busyness.

The tragedy of this not-living is the way children are rushed into it. Cummings is by no means the first person to recognize that Americans force their children to grow up much more rapidly than most other peoples of the world. Parents live in the constant fear that childhood misdemeanors will mean adult failure. They concentrate great quantities of attention on their offspring, but the effect of this concentration is to foreshorten the experience of being young and to hurry children into "pu . . . tres . . . cen . . . ce." The wonderfully suggestive last lines of the poem summarize Cummings' point. The French can take time to lull their children to sleep with nursery songs like "fais do-do" (go to sleep). Americans, by contrast, teach their children the virtue of speed in order that they will be able to live the adult credo, "fais do" (make dough) or "fais do . . . re . . . [mi]" (make money) or, possibly even, "fais do" (save money by making-do).

When they have learned by imitation, Cummings suggests, the children will, like their present neighbors, find that the spirit of business-like speed and efficiency, implicit in such abbreviations as "do" (ditto) and "re" (regarding), will even invade the leisurely joy of making babies. They will have learned to be merely undead like the flowerless and odorless rubber plant in the hotel lobby. They will be dissatisfied, even bored, with their "lives." Every "now" will be a "mean. . .while": that is, every moment will be mean or inferior because it is merely an interim before a better (hopefully) moment. They will even have lost the ability to feel genuinely the "k/ingly" comfort of riding an elevator.

Children, on the other hand, live by a wholly different time scheme. Their world is forever now. Depending upon others for their physical needs, they do not plan for their future; they yield themselves to immediate experience. To them life is not a problem to be solved but a gift to be received. They do not impose their wills on it; they open themselves to receive it as it is.

The difference between childhood and adulthood is quite real and fundamental. Consider the adult's command of language. Fearing for his life, the caveman developed a warning system, the beginning of what we call "language." The function of this system was—and is—to simplify and control life for the comfort and safety of man. Thus, we can imagine the caveman grouping all the events in his experience which threatened destruction and calling them, "owch." He yelled "owch" whenever he detected signs of landslides, rattle-snakes, mastodons, lightning, or poison ivy. When wife and neighbor cavemen heard the cry of "owch," their lives depended upon their rapidly discarding 99% of their perceptions of the diverse, chaotic world about them, and responding to the single idea: Trouble!

Modern civilization is simply a complicated refinement of "owch." It has resulted from a long process of making distinctions, throwing away excess experience, and grouping what is important, convenient, or useful according to human purposes. Modern man needs to distinguish mastodons from poison ivy as different varieties of trouble; the process of reduction and simplification is, however, fundamentally the same today as it was eons ago. The world, as adults know it, then, is really a mirror of their own needs. When we speak of something's making sense, we really mean that it fits the system by which we conveniently "live our lives." Thus, putting it the other way round, Cummings has said, "if babyish nonsense bores you stiff, you have 'civilization.' "

Children, precisely because they are not yet civilized, see and hear beyond what they can conceptualize and "understand." Although it may seem nonsense to adults, the knowledge of children comes directly from pulsating, unsystematic actuality. One must, for example, be a child to know the nonsense truth of stanza five in "meanwhile" that trains chew. Adults will puzzle over what trains have in common with eating. But children know that trains chew, because children do not *understand* so much as they *hear,* and they *hear* trains—"chewing."

The quality of mind that hears a word like "chewing" instead of merely understanding it (and *feels* that a train "jerk.ilyr,ushes") is alive and open. And one of the reasons that Cummings values it so highly is that it is open to people as well as to sounds and smells and to the feel of elevators sinking and then gliding. The child, in the poem, with comical difficulty, dresses for the night. Then, in a burst of pleasure, he presents himself: "See!" The adult, responding to the job done—awkwardly and slowly at that—and not to the child, answers, "so long." Again, when adults meet other adults in elevators, they turn "sin"fully false smiles on each other, smiles designed precisely to inhibit rather than to initiate a fresh and genuine human relationship. Small wonder that the smiles sink with the sinking elevator: only the genuine stands a chance of survival.

Cummings knew that children cannot serve as an ultimate standard of value. He was not so totally naive as he often pretended to be. He was uniquely sensitive to children, but his very sensitivity implied an honest understanding of childhood's limits. The other side of the child's commitment to the world of present sense, for example, is his monstrous egoism. In an article

for *Vanity Fair* in 1926, Cummings wrote about tabloid newspapers as symbols of infantile America.[2] Celebrating "a climax
in the orgiastic worship of the present tense of the verb To Be,"
Cummings said, tabloids reflect the typical trait of childhood—its
illimitable egoism. America, he concluded, had grown downhill
from the Pilgrim Fathers to a "great Big Egoistic Baby." In other
contexts, as we have seen, Cummings acclaimed the traits of
childhood which adults have lost. In his best works, he combined
both views of children. He neither overestimated nor underestimated their value as spiritual and cultural yardsticks.

A poem called "Christmas Tree" [*Poems 1923-1954,* p. 141],
which Cummings once published in a separate volume, gets its
special intensity from the fullness with which Cummings entered
into the mind and heart and even the speech patterns of the
child-speaker. At the same time, however, the poem does not
insist that the reader fully accept the child's point of view. The
poem is a child's sensitive sympathy for another being. The
sympathy is, however, impure and, directed as it is toward a
Christmas tree, at least excessive; and still, it is innocently
profound.

Addressing the Christmas tree directly, the child yearns to
comfort a being which is lonely and lost and, as the child sees
it, separated from its mother. He tries to cure its pain by
acting toward it as a parent would. He offers to hug the tree
into a sense of safety and then to make it proud and happy by
dressing it in Christmas decorations and standing it in a window
for everyone to admire. Clearly, the child speaks from his own
knowledge of loneliness and fear. As he opens the box of decorations, he says:

> look   the spangles
> that sleep all the year in a dark box
> dreaming of being taken out and allowed to shine,
> the balls the chains red and gold the fluffy threads,

The child's own fear of the dark adds a special poignancy to
his description of the box of decorations. And yet, as the poem
moves to its climax, an important quality of irony qualifies the
value of the child's love. As he prepares to decorate the tree,
the child says:

put up your little arms
and i'll give them all to you to hold
every finger shall have its ring
and there won't be a single place dark or unhappy

then when you're quite dressed
you'll stand in the window for everyone to see
and how they'll stare!
oh but you'll be proud

These lines truly represent the quality of a child's imagination,
but the child is not to be mistaken for E. E. Cummings. The
child is transformed by the spirit of giving, but he speaks the
language of American materialism. To love here means to shower
with gifts. To be happy is to be gaudily dressed and to be
admired by everyone. The lines indeed recall the earlier ones
in which the child says, "i will comfort you/because you smell
so sweetly." The "because" here is revealing. In the child's
mind, as in his parents', love is something to bestow only on
the deserving; a commodity, it is part of a system of rewards
and punishments. The poem captures a child's mind in a
moment of instinctive love, accurately and without sentimen-
tality; the quality of that love, in both its instinctiveness and
its meretriciousness, implicitly indicts a culture.

One of Cummings' best children poems is a street-corner
anecdote about a Salvation Army band. A child appears at the
end to produce a surprising denouement, which illustrates in a
single moment much of what has been said so far about Cummings' use of children.

the skinny voice

of the leatherfaced
woman with the crimson
nose and conquettishly-
cocked bonnet

having ceased   the

captain
announces that as three
dimes seven nickels and ten
pennies have been deposited upon

the drum there is need

of just twenty-five cents
dear friends
to make it an even
dollar   whereupon

the Divine Average who was

attracted by the inspired
sister's howling moves
off
will anyone tell him why he should

blow two bits for the coming of Christ Jesus

?
? ?
? ? ?
!

nix, kid

[*Poems 1923-1954*, p. 145]

The speaker in this poem is a tough, disaffected cynic. His description of the Salvation Army representatives effectively reveals the fallen state of Christian service. The woman with "the skinny voice" wears her bonnet in imitation of the sex queens who smile invitingly at America from the soft-drink and soap advertisements; the captain adopts the tactics of the auctioneer and the sidewalk pitchman. In the next moment, however, the speaker bitingly satirizes the proud, salesman-proof lovelessness of the man in the street who, it was once hoped, would speak with the voice of God.

Having used spacing instead of punctuation earlier in the poem, Cummings now inserts a series of punctuation marks, which are highly expressive. The question marks suggest the speaker's highly ambivalent emotions. They suggest his growing, if cynical, pleasure in having analyzed the crowd correctly (none comes forward to give even the requested two bits). They suggest also his plaintive hope that someone will respond to the inspired message implicit in the skinny voice (compare "the inspired/sister's howling" with "the sister's inspired howling." The placement of the adjective serves a double function: without the slightest qualification, it insists that the sister has a terrible voice; at the same time, however, it insists also that she is in fact inspired). The question marks suggest, finally, the speaker's indecision about his own obligations. The speaker in his moment of crisis is a fitting image of modern man who remembers the gospel of love, who can even use it to evaluate his surroundings, but who cannot bring himself to believe and to act.

Suddenly, the question marks are answered by an exclamation point. A child appears out of the crowd! Lacking the sophistication of the adult, inexperienced with fraud, insensitive to the corrupted voice of Christianity, the child responds in love to the inherent and eternal message. The child's gesture moves the speaker to a gesture of his own. Instinctively, he steps forward to try to protect the child from being a sucker. Adopting the slang of the Divine Average (compare the speaker's own educated diction and syntax in "whereupon/the Divine Average who was/attracted by the inspired/sister's howling moves/off"), the speaker takes it upon himself to indoctrinate the child into twentieth-century faithlessness. Paradoxically, however, the act itself affirms the very values which his advice denies; for his is an act of compassion, an act which acknowledges the obligations of universal brotherhood. A child's immediate, impulsive, unsophisticated responsiveness moves an adult to a believably complex rediscovery of what it means to be human. Simultaneously comic and pathetic, the poem is an unsentimental comment on the continuing possibility of love in the modern world.

II *Detachment*

Cummings admired children's playful detachment from the world at least as much as their direct responsiveness to it. These two reactions are equally indifferent to the ordinary concerns of adults, and they were therefore equally serviceable to Cummings' critique of contemporary culture. But Cummings' enchantment with the spirit of play was more than negative. He was close to total seriousness when he once suggested that Congress pass a bill "compelling every adult inhabitant of the United States of America to visit the circus at least twice a year." If such a law passed, he predicted, four out of five hospitals, jails, and insane-asylums would close down.[3] His theory—and it informs much of his own esthetic—was that circus performers play with life in a way which removes audiences from their preoccupation with the "bigness of their littleness"—with themselves, their jobs, their neighbors, and their golf games—and carries them to a vision of their humanity. An aerial somersault is a design in space in which the aerialist literally plays with living, creating beauty in apparent disregard of possible consequences. Comparing aerialist Ernest Clark's "triple somersaulting, double-twisting and reverse flights" with paintings by El Greco, Cummings found both communicating a supreme sense of aliveness. The very detachment of children and artists from the ordinary problems of physical survival testifies to the vitality of the life which is beyond survival. Cummings is essentially a comic poet, and one of his most common techniques is to approach serious matters of politics, religion, social customs and behavior, life, and death in the spirit of a child's imaginative play.

A poem which begins, "(of Ever-Ever Land i speak," [*Poems 1923-1954*, p. 335], for example, arraigns the whole of modern life. It attacks the twentieth century's godless worship of a high standard of living, its understanding of life in its scientific but not its spiritual dimensions, its preoccupation with sex to the exclusion of love, its brutal prejudices, its habits of conformity. The poem phrases the attack with such playfulness, however, that the reader must laugh even as he simultaneously shakes his head in sadness. The setting, announced in the first line, echoes explicitly the world of the nursery. So too does the language which describes Ever-Ever Land as a place "that's as simple as simple can be." The same childlike play suffuses the poem's inversion of Milton's famous homily, "They also serve who only stand and wait." After announcing his subject, the poet invites his audience ("sweet morons") to gather around and then adds, "who does not dare to stand or sit/may take it lying down." In similar fashion the last stanza trifles with Kipling's famous line, "A woman is only a woman, but a good cigar is a smoke." Cummings' version is:

(but only sameness is normal
in Ever-Ever Land
for a bad cigar is a woman
but a gland is only a gland)

The same spirit speaks even through the climactic line which comments on Nazi Germany's incredibly brutal treatment of Jews. Ever-Ever Land, says the poet, is a place "where it's lucky to be unlucky/ and the hitler lies down with the cohn." The poem as a whole makes a series of very serious allegations against the contemporary world, and yet the tone finally rises above the evil and above indignation, and with an eye to the farthest possible horizon, says, "I don't care."

Cummings achieves his sophisticatedly infantile play through a variety of techniques in varying combinations. He juxtaposes vastly dissimilar ideas. The results are wonderfully imaginative notions, such as a world which is "probably made of roses & hello." He exaggerates fantastically. The apogee is a delightful little poem which begins:

who knows if the moon's
a balloon, coming out of a keen city
in the sky—filled with pretty people?
                    [*Poems 1923-1954*, p. 103]

and concludes its delineation of the heavenly city with the notation that:

always
    it's
        Spring)and everyone's
in love and flowers pick themselves

There are wildly imaginative contradictions. Strung together they compose Cummings' well-known poem "as freedom is a breakfastfood." Two lines are: "as hatracks into peachtrees grow" and "or mountains are from molehills made."

Finally, many of Cummings' poems seem clothed in childhood because of purely verbal play which sets off the poet's inspired nonsense. Influenced by nothing so much as children's counting rhymes ("One potato two potato three potato four/five potato six potato seven potato more"), Cummings' magnificently alert ear could turn Benjamin Franklin's famous axiom into "early to better is wiser for worse" and, in the process, entice otherwise staid readers into standing on their heads. He delightedly invents words, discovers aural puns, and generally kicks up his heels, frisking with the sounds and appearances of words, disdaining their dictionary limitations.

The poem "what if a much of a which of a wind" includes all of these techniques. The special quality that results can be illumined by comparing it to the seventeenth-century English poet Andrew Marvell's "To His Coy Mistress." Marvell's poem, like Cummings', develops a highly imaginative world of "if" through a series of gay exaggerations:

> Had we but world enough, and time,
> This coyness, Lady, were no crime.
> We would sit down and think which way
> To walk and pass our long love's day.
> Thou by the Indian Ganges' side
> Shouldst rubies find; I by the tide
> Of Humber would complain. I would
> Love you ten years before the Flood,
> And you should, if you please, refuse
> Till the conversion of the Jews.

Cummings' exaggerations have an extra helping of playfulness, however, not only because they are quantitatively bigger, but because Cummings' exploitation of words simply as words suggests the special exuberance of children. Cummings' first stanza reads:

> what if a much of a which of a wind
> gives the truth to summer's lie;
> bloodies with dizzying leaves the sun
> and yanks immortal stars awry?
> Blow king to beggar and queen to seem
> (blow friend to fiend: blow space to time)
> —when skies are hanged and oceans drowned,
> the single secret will still be man
>   [*Poems 1923-1954,* p. 401]

"What if . . ." is a child's question. "What if a much of a which of a wind" is both a child's effort to find the right superlative and his pure delight in the sounds of words. The notion of a wind which might blow a king to a beggar is, as hyperbole goes, conventional enough, but the imp is at work in blowing "queen to seem" and peculiarly so in blowing "friend to fiend." The "r" blown from "friend" is a visual demonstration of the ease with which this particular wind can blast the world into topsy-turvy.

The same breezy gaiety which testifies to the inherent importance of man beneath modernism's encrusted idiocies in "what if a much of a which of a wind" insists upon the idiocies in the following sonnet:

> when serpents bargain for the right to squirm
> and the sun strikes to gain a living wage—
> when thorns regard their roses with alarm
> and rainbows are insured against old age
>
> when every thrush may sing no new moon in
> if all screech-owls have not okayed his voice
> —and any wave signs on the dotted line
> or else an ocean is compelled to close
>
> when the oak begs permission of the birch
> to make an acorn—valleys accuse their
> mountains of having altitude—and march
> denounces april as a saboteur
>
> then we'll believe in that incredible
> unanimal mankind(and not until)
> [*Poems 1923-1954*, pp. 441-42]

Even without specific allusion to childhood, the natural world that is freely developed in terms of human conventions suggests a childlike imagination. The nonsense comparisons are loosely added to one another in an infinitely extendible series. Nature is delightfully conceived as if separated from its most essential qualities. Even the artfully awkward syntax, rhythm, and rhyme of "when every thrush may sing no new moon in" contributes to the poet's innocent delight—one that exists simultaneously with his horror of a society seriously awry.

Sometimes Cummings' verbal play serves no serious purpose

whatever. Cummings has used it indeed in some of the best light verse written in the twentieth century. One highly elliptical but vastly amusing poem represents a melancholic New Yorker whose gloomy expectations produce their own fulfillment. The poem can be read in several ways. One is to imagine the man walking down a city street, talking to himself, making an effort to speak to the vision of loveliness which moves by him, stuttering in his effort to say to himself and to it everything that suddenly demands to be said, and finally trailing off in defeat as he watches the lovely rear of his vision disappear in the crowd and realizes, too late, that New York has values which are at least the equal of Europe's.

>   hanged
>
>   if n
>   y in a real hot spell
>   with o
>
>   man
>
>   what bubbies going
>   places on such
>   babies aint plenty
>   good enough for
>
>   i
>
>   eu*
>   can have
>   you
>
>   rope

[*Poems 1923-1954*, p. 341]

Cummings' playful technique adds immeasurably to the amusing spectacle of the New Yorker's suddenly awakened lechery and final, helpless stare. Even the "hanged . . . rope" frame adds comic overtones. "Hanged if . . ." is, of course, an appropriate

---

* A prefix meaning good. Thus: *eu*-can! as well as "you can" and "Eu-rope."

slang expression by which the speaker can introduce himself and his cheerlessness. And "rope" appropriately signifies the speaker's realization that opportunity has knocked and that he was so sealed off by his own sadness that he didn't hear it in time. Together, however, the two words suggest in addition the popular saying, "Give him enough rope and he'll hang himself," and the reader is left with the ironic comment that the melancholy New Yorker was hanged before he started and is left endlessly taking more rope.

Another poem satirizes the Catholic sisterhood, but its malice is so qualified by playful gaiety that it would be difficult for anyone to take offense:

>   nouns to nouns
>
>   wan
>   wan
>
>   too nons too
>
>   and
>   and
>
>   nuns two nuns
>
>   w an d
>   ering
>
>   in sin
>
>   g
>   ular untheknowndulous s
>
>   pring

[*Poems 1923-1954*, p. 365]

Insisting upon the nuns' attitude of deadly determined denial (they are inactive things, "nouns," as opposed to verbs, and they are a pair of nothings, "nons"), the poem contrasts the two black, shapeless images of sterile passivity with the magically ecstatic vitality of sss - - - pring! But the tone of the poem is completely dominated by the comically not-quite-puns: "noun," "non," "nun"; by the outrageous invention of "untheknown-dulous"; and by the delightful revelation of the plastic qualities of the word "wandering." The two wan-looking nuns walk together, shoulder to shoulder. Together, "wan" and "wan" make two (nuns). Together also, "wan" plus "and" make "wand." It is not entirely clear whether the magic wand of spring causes the nuns to wander without being aware that wandering is a highly appropriate spring activity; or whether, because they have not really responded to spring at all, they do not quite add up to a "w an d"; or whether E. E. Cummings simply enjoyed the visual symmetry of his construction. Clearly, however, if they could speak their own thoughts, the sisters would pronounce the "sin/g"ing mystery of spring a "sin" and their own meandering in it, an "er[r]ing." The poem as a whole permits the reader the deliciously naughty sensation of making fun of a (literally) sacred institution; yet, finally, it is a fun that neither intends nor does harm to anyone.

Although Cummings qualified his valuation of childhood as such, the quality of childlikeness remained one of his major strategies of revelation. It is a strategy with a peculiar appropriateness for an American poet. Americans are famous for the way they enthrone children. Children dominate the conversation at the dinner table. They occupy, to a remarkable degree, the center of the nation's attention. And yet, in marked contrast to tradition-centered societies, Americans tend neither to understand nor to appreciate children for what they are. If a Japanese boy falls down and cries, his mother immediately picks him up and comforts him. He is a child; he feels pain; he needs cheer. If an American boy falls down and cries, his mother is very likely to tell him to get up and stop crying like a baby. If she does go to him, she will, at the very least, worry about whether she is encouraging him to grow up a sissy. He is a child; he feels pain; but he is going to be a man soon, and he must learn how to take his bumps if he is to make his mark in the world.

The roots of these contrasting attitudes lie deep in history. Clearly, however, the American approach stems, in part, from the simultaneous development of the American nation and of mankind's power to control its destiny. A thousand years ago men knew their weakness. They needed feudal lords for protection. The lords needed fortress homes. People needed each other.

They lived on the kind of margin which permitted them to know both the sternness and the goodness of God. Today, after the vast growth of commerce and technology, Americans feel confident in their unaided selves. The widespread use of glass in home building testifies to their sense of being at home in the physical world. A glass wall denies that a house is a fortress against unfriendly forces and encourages instead a sense of universal neighborliness. Instead of being temporary visitors in a world which is not their own, Americans assume they are major stockholders in a world they themselves made. The result is that their children are taught to behave rather like owners with an obligation to improve their property than like house guests with a brief opportunity to sup at another's table.

T. S. Eliot spoke of this false but growing assumption of power when, in the opening lines of "The Dry Salvages," he spoke of the Mississipi River and the nation's changing attitude toward it.

> I do not know much about gods; but I think that the river
> Is a strong brown god—sullen, untamed and intractable,
> Patient to some degree, at first recognized as a frontier;
> Useful, untrustworthy, as a conveyor of commerce;
> Then only a problem confronting the builder of bridges.
> The problem once solved, the brown god is almost forgotten
> By the dwellers in cities . . .

Eliot is more impressed than Cummings was with nature, the destroyer of life; the poetry of both men, however, reflects their deep distress about the people who have been so comfortable for so long that they have forgotten the ultimate source of both life and death—people who, at most, perceive life as a solvable problem rather than as a gift.

When Cummings adopted the mask of the child, therefore, he did so in order to remind us what it feels like to be small and powerless, and to receive, and then to give, not in payment, but in spontaneous gratitude. A poet is not a teacher; yet Cummings sought to sensitize us so that we could see and respond to nature and people, to the variegated sights, sounds, and smells of God-given experience, in love, in laughter, and in gladness. His poems invite us to discover experientially the inner meaning of Jesus' warning to his disciples: "Verily I say unto you, Whosoever

For of Such Is the Kingdom

shall not receive the kingdom of God as a little child, he shall
not enter therein." Cummings would encourage us to say with
him:

> i thank You God for most this amazing
> day:for the leaping greenly spirits of trees
> and a blue true dream of sky;and for everything
> which is natural which is infinite which is yes
>
> (i who have died am alive again today,
> and this is the sun's birthday;this is the birth
> day of life and of love and wings:and of the gay
> great happening illimitably earth)
>
> how should tasting touching hearing seeing
> breathing any—lifted from the no
> of all nothing—human merely being
> doubt unimaginable You?
>
> (now the ears of my ears awake and
> now the eyes of my eyes are opened)

[*Poems 1923-1954,* p. 464]

CHAPTER 3

The Discipline of Giving

"Sex is God-given, and man realizes himself through it."
—Roger Shinn, Union Theological Seminary

ONE OF the few affirmative moments in Cummings' account of his trip to Russia is a description of a girl sunbathing, nude to the waist. The atmosphere of the book as a whole is overwhelmingly close and restrictive. Entering Russia is like entering a dark, small, airless dungeon, and then hearing the door slam behind. Political doctrine is everywhere, and everywhere it circumscribes and stifles the minds and the hearts of the people. Near the end of his trip, however, Cummings one day catches a glimpse of an unknown sunbather. His leaping excitement reflects the intensity of his previous sense of suffocation. The girl appears completely conscious of her sex, proud of it, and yet at the same time relaxed and, even, innocent. She is a free spirit.[1]

In the light of Cummings' whole career, it is not surprising that the image of a semi-nude girl should have been so full of meaning; for sex was, from his earliest work, one of his two or three favored subjects. Because of his persistent interest Cummings was, on occasion, accused of being obsessed with sex and of being merely adolescent in his insistence on talking about an area of experience which mature people know about but do not feel obliged to talk about constantly.

To some degree, the accusation was fair. Cummings used sexual relations as a banner with which to lead the world to a new start, to marshal the faithful into a revolutionary attack on the establishment. In poems about prostitutes and barflies, about venereal disease and the sex act itself, he often seemed merely crude, like a child shouting obscenities at his elders.

On the other hand, the very persistence with which Cummings treated the subject of sex demands that we consider his intention and his achievement carefully and respectfully. If he wrote bad poems about sex, he also wrote some very good ones. His best sex poems reflect his careful attention to the subject over many years. They reflect his profound contemplation of sexual experience in its many manifestations. They reflect his study of the way in which sexual experience illuminates modern American life. They reflect, finally, his persistent effort to discover a poetic style appropriate to his subject.

I *Early Traditionalism*

Cummings certainly had some of the impulses of a rebel, and yet the striking feature of the early sex poems is their traditionalism. The long poem, "Epithalamion" for example, begins:

> Thou aged unreluctant earth who dost
> with quivering continual thighs invite
> the thrilling rain the slender paramour
> to toy with thy extraordinary lust,
> (the sinuous rain which rising from thy bed
> steals to his wife the sky and hour by hour
> wholly renews her pale flesh with delight)
> —immortally whence are the high gods fled?
>   [*Poems 1923-1954*, p. 3]

The sparing use of capitalization and punctuation and, infrequently, a fresh choice of words remind us that the poem does not appear in an anthology of sixteenth- or seventeenth-century English verse. Everything else about the poem is traditional in the extreme. The very idea of a wedding song, regular stanza forms, rhyme scheme, archaic diction, grammatical inversions, the formal address to nature—all announce a poet steeped in tradition. Yet, again, the authentic Cummings impulse is present. The poem as a whole is a call for man to awake from his slumber, to rediscover the vitality of life. The gods of old were lusty souls, as were the minds that conceived them, Cummings reminds us; modern man seems to have forgotten that he is

alive. But the earth remains as a means of rediscovery. No sim-
pering Victorian female she, insisting that "leg" is too vulgar a
word and that "limb" is but a more or less decorous compromise.
On the contrary, the first stanza presents the earth as a sensual,
adulterous woman from whom the virile rain returns to his law-
ful wife the sky. For modern man, "still the mad magnificent
herald Spring/ assembles beauty from forgetfulness." To be
wholly alive he must escape the merely comfortable life of light
bulbs, furnaces, and razorblades and reestablish his fundamental
connection with nature.

Many poems from all stages of Cummings' career are similarly
cast in traditional modes. Repeatedly, Cummings celebrated the
lusty and the uninhibited in terms which echo earlier English
poetry. He frequently used the traditional *carpe diem* (seize the
day) situation: a man attempting to persuade his lady love to
bed with him because life is short, and death, final. And, in the
manner of Herrick or Waller, he used the diction of the aristo-
cratic courtier.

II *Experiments*

The most instructive feature of the early poems, however, is
that Cummings was never entirely comfortable in the traditional
mode, and he experimented tirelessly to find his own unique
fusion of the traditional and the modern. He was capable of
writing too many tired, pale, painfully awkward lines like:

> Each tapering breast is firm and smooth
> that in a lovely fashion doth
> from my lady's body grow;
>> [*Poems 1923-1954*, p. 18]

No wonder he was moved to experiment.

One early effort, "Thy fingers make early flowers of all things,"
[*Poems 1923-1954*, p. 11], varies from the traditional *carpe diem*
poem so slightly that it almost escapes notice. Much of its special
tenderness, however, results from Cummings' having reversed the
usual male-female roles. The maiden is a coquette, but her
intentions are far more openly dishonorable than those of her
seventeenth-century sisters. Far from putting her suitor off, she

is gently leading him out of his fearful preoccupation with life's evanescence, encouraging him to put his whole heart into his kissing. "listen/ beloved/i dreamed" [*Poems 1923-1954*, p. 26], presents the male speaker subtly but traditionally threatening his lady. But here archaic and modern colloquial diction intermix, and the apparently traditional imagery communicates with special force through its association with fantastic Freudian dream material.

Another experiment produced one of Cummings' most famous poems, "O sweet spontaneous/earth." A sophisticated, rather literary speaker meditates about the earth, distinguishing between an abstract and a natural attitude toward it:

> O sweet spontaneous
> earth how often have
> the
> doting
>
>   fingers of
> prurient philosophers pinched
> and
> poked
>
> thee
> , has the naughty thumb
> of science prodded
> thy
>
>   beauty   how
> often have religions taken
> thee upon their scraggy knees
> squeezing and
>
> buffeting thee that thou mightest conceive
> gods
>   (but
> true
>
> to the incomparable
> couch of death thy
> rhythmic
> lover

        thou answerest

      them only with

          spring)
          [*Poems 1923-1954*, pp. 39-40]

   The poem deserves attention insofar as it clearly reveals Cummings' intentions. Its inherent worth, however, has been considerably overrated. It is an interesting poem rather than a good one. Despite its experiments, the poem never quite gets off the level of flat statement.

   Cummings presents philosophy, science, and theology as dirty old men disgustingly attempting to recapture their lost youth. They are victims of what Cummings called, in his Harvard lectures, "mental concupiscence." Their specific ills are their effort to reduce life to abstractions and their underlying effort to make life conform to the purposes of man. From this kind of desire earth withholds her charms. By contrast, the natural relationship of earth and death issues in the spontaneous vitality of SPRING. The arrangement of the poem on the page is Cummings' experimental effort to represent his theme. Negatively, it is a rebuff to literary conventions (which parallel the conventions of philosophy, science, and theology). Positively, it forces us to a dramatic sense of the poem's meaning. The clearest instance is the placement of "spring." The wide spaces separating the last three lines function as musical rests of varying length. The consequence is a great sudden stress on the word "spring," so that, in effect, it springs at us.

   The odd punctuation functions similarly. The comma at the beginning of the line ",has the naughty thumb," for example, forces us to hold the previous clause in mind an instant longer than we expected to. Or, to use a musical analogy again, the comma forces a rest on the first beat of a new measure instead of the expected downbeat. Dramatically, the effect is a *sense* of a prurient philosopher's poke. The comma may even be a visual image of such a poke.

   In a way which is, in the conventional sense of the term, clear—and yet poetically not very impressive—Cummings here used sex as a symbol of uninhibited spontaneity, of natural vitality in contrast to sterile human conventionality. It is a rather blunt instrument, however; and, at the least, Cummings left undefined the relationship between sex and death. The poem says that true vitality results from a relationship with death which is, somehow, like the cycle of the seasons. The nature of the relationship, however, is by no means clear. Cummings' best poems about sex fully and precisely render this relationship.

III   *Extending the Implications*

At the same time that Cummings experimented with both traditional and original poetic modes with which to treat the subject of sex, he experimented also with ways of extending the implications of his subject. Many of his poems identifying sex and nature dramatize a highly generalized *joie de vivre*. The negative side of this attitude, also highly general, is his attack on philosophy, science, and religion in "O sweet spontaneous/earth." Other poems approach these same targets more concretely; still others add new targets.

Professor Josiah Royce of Harvard, for example, is a specific prurient philosopher" in a poem in which he stars opposite a stripteaser named Dolores [*Poems 1923-1954*, p. 169]. The performer, completely conscious of herself, ignorant but with a body "keen chassised like a Rolls/Royce," removes her clothes for the pleasure of a responsive audience. Professor "Royce rolls" down Kirkland Street, alone, totally engrossed in his ideas, absent-mindedly having forgotten his necktie. We do not need a Freudian interpretation of Professor Royce to see that, totally caught up in his own intellectual abstractions, he has forgotten the source of life as well as his necktie.

Like many American artists from Walt Whitman and Thomas Eakins to William Faulkner and Jackson Pollock, Cummings had a lingering suspicion about the validity even of art itself. Whitman claimed that the world was the only real poem, that his creations were but pale imitations whose justification lay in their potential for returning readers to the world with renewed vision. Similarly, Cummings writes of a naked woman: "painting wholly feels ashamed/before this music, and poetry cannot/go near because perfectly fearful" [*Poems 1923-1954*, p. 122]. Like science and philosophy and theology, art too destroys what it touches.

The sin of sexlessness is by no means limited to the intellectual élite, however. It is one of the defining characteristics of "most-people"—businessmen, politicians, soldiers (especially generals), old maid aunts, students. The list is infinitely extendible, for the sin of sexlessness is conventionality; and conventionality, the separation of a person from himself, is omnipresent. A sonnet, "whereas by dark really released" [*Poems 1923-1954*, p. 113], for example, contrasts a fashionable lady by night and by day. At night, Cummings suggests, she is what women inherently are: she is passionately alive. Freed from the manners and customs which imprison her by day, freed perhaps from the foundation garments which symbolize her larger cultural prison, she expresses her sexuality with the savage delight of a lady wrestler. By day —which is to say, most of the time—she is merely the ghost of her true self. Instead of "terrific fingers which . . . joke/on my passionate anatomy" she approaches people with "just/a half-smile (for society's sweet sake)." Instead of lips which "study/my head gripping for a decision" she paints her mouth with a precisely calculated, Helena Rubinstein-approved touch of "invitation." At night she is healthily aggressive; by day she is an obscenity. Her perfume, like her lipstick, bespeaks a deracinated sexuality: the aroma is inviting, but it is an invitation to sexlessness. The poem speaks with savage satire about the society whose "mind-forged manacles" inhibit human beings from being whole.

IV Sex and the Humanization of Modern Life

We would underestimate Cummings greatly, however, if we concluded that his poetry is merely a testament to the sensual, primitive, uninhibited life and merely a critique of social and intellectual conventions. At least two important qualifications need to be added to this view. The first is that Cummings does not always take himself quite so seriously as do most writers about sex. In a famous essay written in 1938,[2] a French journalist, Raoul de Roussy de Sales, commented that "America appears to be the only country in the world where love is a national problem." The French, he added, tend to think of love as a comical affair because they accept it "as one of those gifts of the gods which one might just as well take as it is: a mixed blessing at times, and at other times a curse or merely a nuisance." But nowhere else in the world than in America "can one find a people devoting so much time and so much study to the question of the relationship between men and women. Nowhere else is there such concern about the fact this relationship does not always make for perfect happiness."

One important dimension of Cummings' treatment of sex is his "unAmerican" recognition that sex, like many other things that Americans take very seriously, has its comic side. Cummings has much too active a risibility to read life as though it were one continuous ridge of excitement. Among those poems which dramatize sexual experience itself, for example, many end comically. "when i have thought of you somewhat too" [*Poems 1923-1954*, p. 119] suggests finally that sex is a delightful release, like a child's innocent play; but it is also a ridiculously brief and unimportant encounter, composed of nine-tenths avaricious expectation and one-tenth love.

The second qualification is more important. One of the primary functions of sex in Cummings' poetry is, to be sure, to judge the characteristics of modern life which Cummings finds inhumanly restrictive—and there are many! But at the same time, the central thematic thrust of the poetry is toward a joyous, spontaneous acceptance of immediate experience; and one of the immediacies of the twentieth century is industrialization. Cummings did not often enough front this problem. In urging people to open their pores to the life that is immediately before them, he was obliged to include modern industrial and commercial life as an object of celebration as well as of contempt. In short, if sex was a valid metaphor for Cummings, we would expect to find him using it, on occasion, to reveal joy in the commonplace as well as horror. And Cummings did, in fact, use sex for precisely this purpose.

"she being Brand" renders a sexual experience and relates it to America's interest in automobiles. The poem exploits automobile argot and, in particular, works out the implications of a car's commonly being referred to as "she." It recounts the frustration of a supposedly knowing driver with a virgin car. He

first floods the carburetor. Later he gets into the wrong gear.
Throughout, the poem comically forces language into double
references; the mood is hilarious.

        she being Brand

        -new;and you
        know consequently a
        little stiff i was
        careful of her and(having

        thoroughly oiled the universal
        joint tested my gas felt of
        her radiator made sure her springs were O.

        K.)i went right to it flooded-the-carburetor cranked her

        up,slipped the
        clutch(and then somehow got into reverse she
        kicked what
        the hell)next
        minute i was back in neutral tried and

        again slo-wly;bare,ly nudg.   ing(my

        lev-er Right-
        oh and her gears being in
        A 1 shape passed
        from low through
        second-in-to-high like
        greasedlightning)just as we turned the corner of Divinity

        avenue i touched the accelerator and give

        her the juice,good

                        (it
        was the first ride and believe i we was
        happy to see how nice she acted right up to
        the last minute coming back down by the Public
        Gardens i slammed on
        the

```
internalexpanding
&
externalcontracting
brakes Bothatonce and

brought allofher tremB
-ling
to a:dead.

stand-
;Still)
```

[*Poems 1923-1954*, pp. 178-79]

If there is a moral of any kind in this poem, the wildly exuberant quality of the humor suggests a double one. On the one hand, it suggests a satirical attack on that particular kind of modern human sterility which cannot distinguish between humans and machines and the appropriate ways of approaching each and which, therefore, treats humans as more or less useful but essentially interchangeable parts. The poem implies that modern man treats his women and his automobiles the same way despite their being wholly different.

Another dimension, however, is Cummings' delighted awareness that the identity of women and cars, suggested by contemporary slang, has an important validity. We need to distinguish in this poem between the attitude of Cummings the poet and that of the driver-speaker. Cummings seems casually gay throughout the poem. He enjoys the narrative and he obviously enjoys the language play. But even the driver contributes a positive tone to the poem. For, while he is unduly confident of his skill at the start and gets his comeuppance when "she" kicks into reverse instead of jumping forward, his confidence is ultimately justified, because it is based on genuine concern and understanding. He is alert to "her" needs, wholly conscious of the way she is reacting. His sense of personal relationship is implicit in his substitution of "believe i we" for the slang expression, "believe you me." The end of the poem, in particular, reflects the driver's joyous sense of the car's complete responsiveness. The delight that suffuses the poem as a whole, Cummings seems to say, is wholly appropriate to both automobiles and human beings. In short, in "she being Brand" sex and technology define each other by identity as well as by contrast.

"i will be" parallels "she being Brand" in its fusing sex and another central aspect of modern life, the city.

                                        i will be
                    M o ving in the Street of her

                    bodyfee l inga ro undMe the traffic of
                    lovely;muscles-sinke x p i r i n g S
                       uddenl
                    Y   totouch
                                   the curvedship of
                                               Her-
                    . . . . kIss   her:hands
                                       will play on,mE as
                    dea d tunes OR s-cra p-y leaVes flut te rin g
                    from Hideous trees or

                    Maybe Mandolins
                                       l oo k-
                       pigeons fly ingand

                    whee(:are,SpRiN,k,LiNg an in-stant with sunLight
                    t h e n)l-
                    ing all go BlacK wh-eel-ing

                    oh
                       ver
                          mYveRylitTle

                    street
                    where
                    you will come,

                                   at twi li ght
                    s(oon & there's
                    a   m oo
)n.

                                        [*Poems 1923-1954*, p. 99]

The poem is the poet's excited anticipation of a meeting with his lover. Chaotically arranged, the words and letters vividly and wittily render the poet's shivery response to his lover's expected caresses. Mounting excitement reaches a climactic transport in the sudden reference to flying pigeons (accompanied by a shift of verb tense from future to present and of pronouns from "her" to "you"). Then, the moment of frenzied passion recedes to a hushed, calm waiting for the actual twilight meeting both of male and female and of day and night.

Critics have cited the pigeon passage to illustrate Cummings' use of imitative typography. SpRiN,k,LiNg" is a visual representation of the sprinkling effect which the pigeons have as they fly through the sun's rays.[3] The passage also illustrates Cummings' interest in simultaneity. The parenthesis in the middle of "wheeling" forces the reader to hold in mind at the same time both the wheeling of the pigeons and their effect on the sunlight. In the context of the whole poem, however, the isolation of the "whee" of "wheeling" and the spasmodic appearance of "sprinkling" imply also the high point of sexual frenzy.

Finally, however, the really significant achievement of the poem is the way Cummings has humanized the contemporary city. Like the paintings of his friend John Marin, Cummings' "i will be" communicates a sense of the excitement and almost tactile vitality of a cityscape. The poem represents an ambitious undertaking, particularly in a nation which has become steadily more urban in fact while remaining essentially agrarian and anti-urban in its values. In it, as well as in "she being Brand," Cummings implies that human fulfillment, symbolized by fully satisfactory sex experience, depends on a responsive acceptance of modern life.

V *Four Portraits of Sex and Death*

Among Cummings' very best sex poems are several portraits. Their success depends on a variety of happy accidents, individual to each poem. But they all have at least one feature in common. All integrate with sexual experience the idea of death. All work out fully the relationship which remained forced and undeveloped in "O sweet spontaneous earth." In the portraits discussed in the following pages, the relation of sex and death point to the spiritual dimension of immediate experience. Bringing the two subjects into sharp focus permitted Cummings to integrate in single poems his interest in the immediate appearance of life and in its deepest meanings. The very fact perhaps that the two subjects point in opposite directions may have spurred him to a vision which was at once carefully observant and deeply understanding, at once complex and whole.

One portrait is a dramatic monologue. It might well be titled, "Portrait of a Dead Whore," for the prostitute speaking to her client, apparently pleased with herself and her world, reveals more about the quality of her life than she realizes.

> raise the shade
> will youse dearie?
> rain
> wouldn't that
>
> get yer goat but
> we don't care do
> we dearie we should
> worry about the rain
>
> huh
> dearie?
> yknow
> i'm
>
> sorry for awl the
> poor girls that
> gets up god
> knows when every
>
> day of their
> lives
> aint you,
>   oo-oo.   dearie
>
> not so
> hard dear
>
> you're killing me
>   [*Poems 1923-1954*, p. 88]

The situation and the woman's comments constitute an implicit criticism of average life. The relaxed way in which this man and this woman can concentrate on matters of sex does, as the woman says, judge adversely the lives of most people. It contrasts sharply with the meaningless regularity and rush of most American homes in the morning. In one sense, then, the whore's sympathy for the "poor girls" that have to get up every morning at inhumanly early hours is justified.

Her explicit sympathy and implicit critique are undermined, however, by what she reveals about the quality of her own life. A symbolic reading of the poem would emphasize the whore's sense of disappointment in the rain, a traditional symbol of death and fertility. It might even discover special significance in the slang reference to goats, a traditional symbol of lust. Even without this level of interpretation, however, the prostitute in the poem reveals herself as dead. She and her client awake to rain. But, despite her disappointment, the prostitute feels compelled to adopt a professional cheerfulness. It is as though she catches herself being human for a moment and then quickly remembers that she is not supposed to be human but a woman of pleasure. What she says carries a hollow ring as the professional and the real responses clash. Once having denied her real self, however, the whore retains her professional composure throughout the rest of the poem; and much of the poem's dramatic thrust depends on the reader's awareness of the increasing discrepancy between the two attitudes.

Mechanically repeating her single term of "endearment" five times, the prostitute insists upon her companion's virility and her own enjoyment until her final "you're killing me" produces a reverberatingly ironic denouement. She invokes a slang overstatement in claiming to be in pain; clearly, she intends also that the pain is the special, pleasurable sort which is supposed to accompany sexual intercourse. Given her professional air, however, it is also clear that she feels neither pleasure nor pain, but is merely saying what her customer wants to hear. In short, at the physical level, no customer can "kill" her. She's already dead. She is professionally incapable of being human.

Sociologically speaking, the male in this poem may be killing his bedmate in the sense that his desire sustains the business of prostitution. On the other hand, she cannot be killed any more spiritually than physically, because spiritually too she is already dead. The placement of the "dearies" suggests that the prostitute's only honest responses are her reactions to the rain and to "the poor girls." Thus, she perceives the sterility of other people's lives but is totally unaware that her strictures apply at least equally to her own. This lack of self-awareness testifies to her fundamental depravity. She not only lives in chains; she is totally unconscious of them. But the final irony is that even her language betrays her, for the death of her soul is implicit in the dead clichés which she relies on to express herself.

By contrast, Cummings' portrait of "Marj" reveals a whore who is very much alive despite her professional competence. Her human vitality expresses itself in the Rabelaisian gesture which she substitutes for the customary ways of communicating contempt. She laughs genuinely. She has an inner serenity which transcends the circumstances of her life. She is physically unattractive; she knows she is surrounded by a world of phonies. Yet she is strong, and the roots of her strength lie in her fundamental humility and her consequent unwillingness to take herself too seriously:

> "life?
>   Listen" the feline she with radishred
> legs said (crossing them slowly) "I'm
> asleep. Yep.   Youse is asleep kid
> and everybody is."   And i hazarded
> "god" (blushing slightly)—"O damn
> ginks like dis Gawd" opening slowlyslowly
> them—then carefully the rolypoly
> voice squatting on a mountain of gum did
> something like a whisper, "even her."
> "The Madam?" I emitted; vaguely watching
> that mountainous worthy in the fragile act
> of doing her eyebrows.—Marj's laughter smacked
> me: pummeling the curtains, drooped to a pur. . .
>
> i left her permanently smiling
>   [*Poems* 1923-1954, p. 166]

Marj is, physically, the sort of woman that Cummings' friend Gaston Lachaise frequently memorialized in sculpture, mountainous yet with a cat-like grace and femininity. She does not believe in life as an article of romantic faith, and her disbelief is no cliché. The youthful "i" of the poem, for example, suspects her sincerity when she insists that no one is really alive, suspects that behind her disclaimer there may lie a layer of conventional illusion. But he is mistaken. And both the "i" of the poem and the reader are left finally with the paradoxical sense that Marj is enormously alive precisely because she has no pretension to being so. In contrast with the Madam of the house she has dignity just because she lays no claim to dignity. She lives because she knows that she is dead.

Two poems about stripteasers neatly parallel these two portraits of prostitutes and extend E. E. Cummings' vision of the role of sex in human life. Marj is sister to Sally Rand. In a poem whose exuberant mood is reminiscent of "she being Brand," Cummings celebrated the famous fan dancer of the 1930's and, in the process, celebrated God and the fundamental nature of life.

out of a supermetamathical subpreincestures
pooped universe(of croons canned
à la vallee and preserved goldfishian gestures)
suddenly sally rand

handsomely who did because she could what the movies try
to do because they can't i mean move
yes sir she jes was which the radio aint(proov
-ing that the quickness of the fand intrigues the fly)

for know all men(χαίρετε) *
as it was in the beginning it(rejoice)
was and ever shall be nor every partialness beats one entirety
neither may shadow down flesh neither may vibration create voice

if therefore among foul pains appears an if emerges a joy let
's thank indecent
god p.s. the most successful b.o.fully speaking concession at the recent
world's fair was the paytoilet

[*Poems 1923-1954*, p. 304]

The poem is full of wild comedy: invented scientific-sounding language, the juxtaposition of quotations from the Bible and

---

* χαίρετε, pronounced kī'-re-te, means "greetings."

traditional forms of greeting with illiteracies and slang, a scrambled magician's cliché, an outrageous pun ("b.o.fully"), amusingly improbable rhymes. The source of Cummings' wild delight was of course Sally Rand, and what impressed him most was that, like Marj, Sally Rand "jes was." Her skill as a performer stemmed from her total lack of illusion and pretension. She produced art from her acceptance of the fundamental indecency of life itself. In Cummings' view she did not create indecency; she merely acknowledged it, just as the motion pictures and radio and the traditional, "dignified" language of religion deny it. Sally Rand is an image of a whole being.

Cummings' gay delight in Sally Rand was not, however, indiscriminate approval of what most people disapprove. Cummings was not even an indiscriminate devotee of the striptease. Presumably his frequent attendance at the National Winter Garden in New York enabled him to make acute critical discriminations which less regular spectators missed. "sh estiffl" presents a close-up of a stripper without Sally Rand's talent and distinguishes sharply between art and the merely obscene:

<pre>
        sh estiffl
        ystrut sal
        lif san
        dbut sth

        epoutin(gWh.ono:w
        s li psh ergo
        wnd ow n,
                    r
        Eve

        aling 2 a
        -sprout eyelands)sin
        uously&them&twi
        tching,begins

        unununun?
        butbutbut??
        tonton???
        ing????
</pre>

```
    —Out-&
            steps;which
    flipchucking
    .grins
    gRiNdS

    d is app ea r in gly
    eyes grip live loop croon mime
    nakedly hurl asquirm the
    dip&giveswoop&swoon&ingly

    seethe firm swirl hips whirling climb to
    GIVE
    (yoursmine mineyours yoursmine
    !
    i( )t)
```
                                    [*Poems 1923-1954*, p. 320]

It is not entirely clear whether the mood of the stripper
changes during the course of her act or whether it is the poet
whose attitude changes. In either case, the poem changes direction sharply in the next to the last stanza. The poem begins in
good-humored pleasure with the techniques of the tease. The
poet is enjoying himself, whether the stripper is or not. But the
tone changes after the girl disappears in glee. Indeed, when she
returns, the whole character of the act changes. Her purpose now
is no longer to tease but to stimulate. But the obvious imitation
of sexual frenzy produces a bitterly ironic quality of horror, for
when the stripper finally stands naked, openly offering what
Hollywood's "It" girl of the 1920's merely implied, she is an
ultimate travesty of love and giving. She has revealed herself
to be a mere "it," inhuman. The empty parenthesis emphasizes
the point: she is an image of nothingness, of total sterility, of
death. The final, single parenthesis suggests that the whole act
is ultimately separated from the life beyond it and defines the
potential value of the rest of life by symbolizing pure negation.

The basic terms of "sh estiffl" are almost identical to those
used by the Jewish theologian Martin Buber in his famous book
I-Thou. Buber distinguishes between two kinds of relationship,
I-Thou and I-It. Cummings makes the same distinction when he
contrasts the stripper's pretense of giving herself to another with

her insistence on the distinction between "yours" and "mine." In effect, she tries to act out an I-Thou relationship and achieves one of I-It.

VI A New Morality

This striking parallel between Cummings and Buber is a forcible reminder that poetry is not created in total isolation; it grows from the impingement of a particular time and place upon a creative mind. It is worth noting further, therefore, that Cummings' interest in sex as a subject for art was no accident. His treatment of it was more significant than anything he could have found readymade in American culture, but his general concern was shared widely.

In the World War I era sex became a *cause celebre* for both American literature and American life. Sexual freedom became a means of protesting against many restrictions in our national life. The thought of Sigmund Freud, for example, found a readier reception in America of the 1920's than anywhere else in the world. Significantly, this reception was at least partially founded on a distortion of Freud. He was understood to have found the source of the world's ills in inhibited sexuality, and he was understood further to have pronounced his blessing upon free sexual expression as the way to individual and social health. Dreiser's difficulty, two decades before, in publishing *Sister Carrie* (because he did not punish his heroine for her violation of sexual mores) was, for many, a symbol of what needed eradication in America. The great enemy was the Puritan.

Clearly, Cummings participated in this sexual revolt. He used sex in his poetry for purposes similar to those of Ernest Hemingway, Sherwood Anderson, Henry Miller, Eugene O'Neill, and many other twentieth-century writers. Some of O'Neill's plays, for example, assume that a truly healthy sexuality was only possible in the simple life of times past or on some primitive South Sea island. As recently as the late 1940's, Rodgers and Hammerstein used a version of this theme in their enormously popular musical, *South Pacific*, particularly in the hit song about an island paradise, "Bali Hai." The central impulse of this literature, to which Cummings contributed, was its critique of the dehumanizing forces in modern life.

Ultimately, however, Cummings pointed beyond sex as a critique of society and beyond sex as a form of primitivism. He pointed beyond self-indulgence to self-discipline based on a new understanding of love. He rendered, in effect, poetic images of a new morality.

The leading theme in Western civilization since the Renaissance has been technology. Western man came out of the Dark Ages when he developed confidence in himself as a builder. The doctrine of progress asserts that man can increasingly understand and control life for his own comfort and well-being. This sense of human power, confirmed by the extraordinary development of science and technology, by the building of new nations and great cities, lies at the root of growing secularization. Man, with a new sense of his own stature in the universe, has lost his sense of dependence on the ultimate power of God. (Cummings once said that America was overrun by gadgets designed to eliminate "every vestige of discomfort and of danger including superfluous hair and the human soul.")

Along with the substitution of man, the builder, for the older image of man, the suffering servant, has come an entirely new structure of values oriented toward human achievement. In the complex world of the twentieth century this shift in the conception of man has produced a new conception even of love and marriage. Marriage is not so much a sacramental relationship as social and economic teamwork, and the happy marriage is the one in which the team functions smoothly. Erich Fromm, whose analysis in a series of recent books parallels Cummings' to a striking degree, has described the marriage team:

> the marriage counselor tells us, the husband should "understand" his wife and be helpful. He should comment favorably on her new dress, and on a tasty dish. She, in turn, should understand when he comes home tired and disgruntled, she should listen attentively when he talks about his business troubles, should not be angry but understanding when he forgets her birthday. All this kind of relationship amounts to is the well-oiled relationship between two persons who remain strangers all their lives, who never arrive at a "central relationship," but who treat each other with courtesy and who attempt to make each other feel better.[4]

The widely decried decline in sexual morality reflects this new conception of the nature of love, for the traditional prohibitions against pre-marital and extra-marital sex play were grounded in a view of marriage as a sacred union; with the newer view of marriage as a team participating in the large task of building a better world, the key test of behavior is whether or not it aids or impedes team efficiency, and the evidence, for example, that pre-marital sexual experience damages post-marital teamwork is, at the very least, not clear.

Of this whole structure of vision and value Cummings made a radical criticism. The fundamental error, as he saw it, is the root idea of man the builder. To it he opposed the idea of man as lover, a genuinely responsible man. Cummings' basic premise was that the man who seeks to understand and control the world cannot at the same time accept and love and give himself to it. For, at bottom, building is a self-centered enterprise; loving is other-centered.

The central category in Cummings' sex poems then is giving. Morality does not depend on where and when a sexual experience occurs; it depends on whether there is participation in a genuine giving. Cummings heaped scorn on those who cannot express themselves sexually because of their preoccupation with social customs; but he had no more use for those who indulge themselves sexually as a badge of achievement. One of his most viciously satirical poems, for example, is directed at a boy of twelve who proudly bases a claim to manhood upon a case of gonorrhea [*Poems 1923-1954*, p. 85]. Cummings would have been utterly contemptuous of the sexual competition that characterizes so much of adolescent dating.

Repeatedly Cummings used sex in his poetry to define the meaning of "to give," and in so doing he offered, experientially, a valuable image of man, society, and life. Among many poems about the sex act itself, one of the best is "much i cannot)." It summarizes vividly and significantly the whole range of Cummings' understanding of sexual experience:

> much i cannot)
> tear up the world:& toss
> it away;or
> cause one causeless cloud to purely grow

> but,never
> doubt my weakness
> makes more than most
> strength(less than these how
>
> less than least flowers of rain)thickly
> i fail slenderly i
> win(like touch all stars or
> to live in the moon
>
> a while)and shall
> carve time so we'll before
> what's death
> come(in one bed.
>
> > [*Poems 1923-1954*, pp. 310-11]

The poem is a dramatic monologue, whose narrative situation is not fully revealed till the last line. The speaker, sexually impotent in the beginning of the poem, reaches a climax at the end, a climax which is a fulfillment simultaneously of power and understanding and love for both speaker and reader.

The speaker's initial impotence[5] is a reflection of contemporary life in many different ways. It reflects the modern world's excessive interest in matters sexual—the girlie magazines, Hollywood's sex queens from Clara Bow to Marilyn Monroe, and the plethora of manuals on how to achieve a satisfactory sex life. In a stanza made complex by the ambiguous relationship between the material within and without the parenthesis, the speaker confesses a weakness which he defines by comparison with the kind of strength which could simply tear up the world like a piece of paper. Initially, that is, he sees his weakness in purely physical, muscular terms. More broadly, the beginning of the poem comments on the general impotence of modern man: with his root assumption that he has displaced the Almighty in his capacity to create the conditions of human fulfillment by himself, he must hold himself wholly responsible for any evidence of failure. The guilt is overwhelmingly burdensome and therefore enervating.

But the speaker is no ordinary man. He has some spiritual insight. The second and third stanzas are his conscious effort to erect or, better, to resurrect himself on a spiritual premise. The conscious effort is a contradiction of the premise itself, but the premise is correct. The speaker acknowledges the ultimate power of God and images this power, paradoxically, in the fragility of growing flowers and floating clouds. Consciously, he tries to convince himself and his lover that his weakness is stronger than the world's conception of strength on the grounds that he is at least *aware* of ultimate strength. The world's muscle men, he argues, including its sexual athletes, are puny because of their pretentiousness.

"thickly/i fail slenderly i/win" brilliantly summarizes the speaker's problem. His diagnosis is perfect: he is a failure when he consciously, intensely desires to be a success; he is a success when he accepts himself as a "slender" failure. At the same time, however, the emphasis that Cummings throws onto the first person pronouns by placing them at the beginning and end of a line, underlines the speaker's continued self-preoccupation, even at the moment that he realizes that self-preoccupation *is* the cause of his weakness.

By the middle of the last stanza, just before the poem's climax, the speaker has reconstructed his confidence to the extent that he imagines himself to have the very God-like strength which produced his utter impotence at the beginning of the poem. Significantly, the figure of carving time is of the same order as tearing up the world: both are images of physical effort, of making and destroying the universe.

But the speaker's self-induced confidence both collapses and leaps forward when for the first time in the poem he considers two new dimensions of experience. The poem has been the speaker's preoccupation with his own capacity and incapacity; suddenly as though by accident, he discovers that neither sex nor life in general is a "doing to" but a "being with." With the sudden introduction of the pronoun "we" he realizes with a shock that he has heretofor been regarding his lover as an object rather than a subject and he has been regarding the experience to which he aspires as a creating rather than a giving. At the same time, again as a kind of half-conscious accident, the speaker discovers that there is one dimension of time that he cannot carve: he cannot extend indefinitely the span of a human life.

This double recognition occurs, as it were, between the second and third lines of the last stanza, and it produces the triumphant finale. The speaker breaks off his line of thought with the interjection, "what's death." It is a moment of transcendence. Fully revealed in all his loveless self-preoccupation, the speaker suddenly perceives the insignificance of death and therefore of himself. His salvation lies in the possibility of a "we" relationship, in love. The final "come(in one bed" is both climax and invitation. The speaker finds sexual and spiritual power simultaneously, not through his self-conscious effort to achieve prowess but through his self-denying readiness to give.

Insofar as "what's death" functions as a question, the poem offers several answers. It means physical death, of course, but it means also spiritual death, of which the poem points to two different varieties. There are those who totally disregard the spiritual dimension of their lives, and then there are those, like the speaker, whose cognitive understanding outruns their full, experiential understanding. Finally, insofar as the last line may be read as an answer to the question which precedes it, the poem invokes the Elizabethan identification of death with sexual intercourse. The speaker's death, in short, is fruitful: he discovers the strength of giving and inherits new life.

Again, Erich Fromm provides a relevant gloss. His definition of mature love almost precisely parallels "much i cannot)" in its assertion that giving is the highest expression of human power. Fromm even cites the sex act in illustration. For the male, the culmination of the sex act is an act of giving. Both literally and in a broader metaphorical sense, Fromm concludes, "He cannot help giving if he is potent. If he cannot give, he is impotent."

Ultimately, then, Cummings' was a disciplined celebration of sexual experience. He called man to life, but not to license. He sang of that state of mind in which a man can give himself completely to another human being, to the world, to experience, and thereby participate in otherness, not for his own sake but for the other's. Cummings demanded of a man that he respond in love to the life which is given in love.

CHAPTER *4*

The Esthetics of Realism

"who pays any attention to the syntax of things will
never wholly kiss you;"

I *Cummingsese*

FOR A man with a thoroughgoing contempt for art criticism,
E. E. Cummings wrote a striking amount of it. His address,
"The New Art," delivered at his Harvard graduation in 1915,
was a serious analysis of what is modern in modern painting,
sculpture, music, and literature.[1] But for the most part, paradoxical as it may sound, Cummings' criticism was remarkably con-
sistent with his dislike of criticism. For when he commented
about art in prose, he did so with a distinctive flair. The tone
of most of his criticism was uncritical, even anti-critical.

His essays in *The Dial* and *Vanity Fair* are full of terms like
"intensely alive" and "irrevocably itself." Gaston Lachaise is
"inherently naif, fearlessly intelligent, utterly sincere." He searches
always for "the truths of nature as against the facts of existence."
Paul Manship, on the other hand, is superior to the average
sculptor—but only "in so far as something which is thoroughly
dead is superior to something which has never been alive."[2] T.
S. Eliot makes his readers come alive.[3] Jean Cocteau's portrait
of Picasso reveals his "uncouth aliveness."[4] John Marin, who
Cummings thought was America's greatest living painter, painted
"a structurally sumptuous irrevocably itself coloured vibration."[5]

Cummings used the same terms whether he was speaking of
artists or their work, the fine arts or popular arts. The Woolworth
building seemed to him magnificently alive, "wriggling upward

like a skyrocket."[6] So did stripteaser June St. Clare's walk. She does not merely walk: she *really* walks, Cummings insisted. She does not move, bounce, or jerk: she "propagates." And to the reader who might think him exaggerating, Cummings replied, "You haven't seen her, or you didn't deserve to."[7] From the painting of Cezanne to the spectacle of Coney Island at night the great function of the best art is to put the viewer in touch with the sources of his human vitality. Art is alive when it opens one's pores or raises the hair on his head, when it permits a man once again to experience life as it actually is rather than as he has accustomed himself to seeing it. "Anyone who has ever begun-to-begin falling seventy feet in the Cyclone roller-coaster at Coney Island knows what I mean."[8]

Cummings blared his likes and dislikes in art with a kind of intuitional fury. He scorned the nicely refined analysis of meaning; he scorned equally the carefully qualified judgment. He insisted always that art must have a certain quality of feeling beyond intellectual analysis. Art is, as he repeatedly said—quoting a line from his play *Him*—"a question of being alive."[9] His highest praise was to note that a work of art is far from being a noun, but rather "a magnificent conjugating largeness, an IS."

II   *"A painter is a poet"*

It would be a great mistake to conclude, however, that Cummings did not think about art, that his criticism was nothing but primitive grunts of acceptance and rejection. Despite appearances to the contrary, his thinking about matters esthetic ran far deeper than the proverbial "I don't know anything about art, but I know what I like." His esthetics were those of an art era. He gathered up most of the leading ideas that motivated not only the literature but the music, painting, sculpture, and architecture of the first half of the twentieth century. He was a fascinatingly representative figure. To understand E. E. Cummings, therefore, we need to see him against the background of modernism in general. For to understand modernism is to see more clearly and intensely the uniqueness of Cummings' poetry as well as his apparently quixotic criticism.

The first thing that Cummings shared with other leading figures of modern art was an intense awareness of the nature of art and the relation of the various mediums to one another. Cummings' decision to analyze four different art forms in his Harvard graduation speech was no accident. He, himself, worked in several different media, notably painting, besides poetry. In his criticism he habitually compared painters, poets, actors, and sculptors. The show at the old National Winter Garden was intensely alive, he once said, in just the same way that Marin, Stravinsky, and Lachaise were alive.[10] And at least once, playfully but with a strain of deep seriousness, he denied that any significant differences separate the arts. For the catalogue of an exhibition of his paintings in Rochester, New York, in 1945, Cummings wrote a dialogue between himself and a hypothetical interviewer:

"Oh yes, one more question: where will you live after this war is over?"
"In China; as usual."
"China?"
"Of course."
"Whereabouts in China?"
"Where a painter is a poet."[11]

Cummings' sense of art as a single, indivisible category led him sometimes to such perceptive remarks about individual works as his comment that the wiry, angular lines in Cocteau's portrait of Stravinsky were visual counterparts of the special quality of the composer's music. Even more important, however, is that Cummings' awareness of the relations among the arts matched the same awareness in many other members of his generation. Cummings' work in painting, as well as poetry, was paralleled in the poetry of Marsden Hartley and Max Weber, who were essentially painters. Charles Demuth tried to translate into visual terms the essential reality of Henry James' fiction. Roy Harris tried similarly to capture Walt Whitman in music. Paul Rosenfeld was only the most outstanding example of a critic who took the entire art world as essentially a single enterprise.

In addition, New York, between 1910 and 1930, repeatedly seemed to encourage cross-fertilization at formal and informal gatherings which brought artists, critics, and estheticians into face-to-face relationships. Sometimes it was a meeting to organize an art exhibition at Alfred Stieglitz' 291 Fifth Avenue studio-gallery; sometimes the purpose was to put together an issue of *The Dial* magazine; sometimes they just got together—at Mabel Dodge's or Alfred Kreymborg's or Paul Rosenfeld's. Whatever the place or the reasons, opportunities proliferated for an extraordinary group of men and women to keep in touch with one another: Wallace Stevens, William Carlos Williams, Marianne Moore, Hart Crane, Maxwell Bodenheim, Carl Van Vechten, Lewis Mumford, Paul Rosenfeld, John Marin, Marsden Hartley, William Zorach, Alfred Stieglitz, Georgia O'Keefe, Aaron Copland, Darius Milhaud, Charles Demuth. And, of course, similar gatherings were always available to the traveling artist at Gertrude Stein's famous salon at 27 rue de Fleurus in Paris.

Of their consciousness of the differences among art media more will be said in the next chapter. Here it is enough to emphasize how deeply poets and painters and composers were conscious of one another. In the light of this consciousness, it is not surprising that Wallace Stevens should have asserted that poets can learn their trade by reading what painters have said about theirs, or that the painter Wassily Kandinsky should have commented that Debussy's impressionist technique "merely accentuates the fact that the various arts of to-day learn from each other and often resemble each other."

III *The New Realism*

What is more surprising is how much a generation of artists agreed about the bond that unified it. Kandinsky affirmed that the major problem in the world of his time was neither social nor political but, fundamentally, spiritual. Seduced by the triumphant rise of science and technology, the Western world, he thought, had come to believe that the only believable truth was what white-robed scientists reported from their laboratories. As Ernest Hemingway said some years later, abstractions like honor and courage had become obscenely unreal. But so also had *things*. If scientists had no ruler with which to measure love, neither was there a litmus paper test for the particularity of a teacup. Laboratories could reveal much about the shape, color, tensile strength, and liquid capacity of a teacup. But, said Kandinsky,

"Cezanne made a living thing out of a teacup, or rather in a teacup he realized the existence of something alive."[12] Science had added a great deal of *knowledge about* the world but, to borrow a distinction that William James used to make, it had reduced man's *acquaintance with* the world. Albert Gleizes and Jean Metzinger, trying to uncover the fundamental springs of cubism, only two years after the first Cubist group show in 1911, commented that the painter's mission is to liberate things from their commonplace appearance.[13] Their view and Kandinsky's, that the central mission of art was to restore the "vital impulse of life," echoed from Munich, Germany, to Paterson, New Jersey, where William Carlos Williams was struggling to produce what he called an art of "the immediate and the actual."

When Cummings insisted that art be intensely alive, he used a rather precious, private language. Yet his fundamental esthetic principle was known and accepted round the world. Its meaning lay deeply embedded in almost one hundred years of revolution in behalf of a new, more "realistic" definition of the relations of art and life. In Europe Courbet initiated a personal rebellion when, in the middle of the nineteenth century, he challenged the traditional, academic insistence that the proper function of art was to beautify the unbeautiful and idealize the unideal. Courbet denied the special propriety of nymphs and angels and scenes from classical history, the Bible, or the heroic past of the French people as subjects for painting. He proposed instead that beauty inhered in life, in the present, in the immediately perceivable and that a painting should capture the facts of the living world.

This realistic impulse, the desire to break through conventional perspectives to reveal life as it really is, has been a central motive for art in the twentieth century. The average museum-goer in the 1960's may have difficulty perceiving anything "realistic" about a Picasso or a deKooning painting; he may have similar difficulty upon first seeing a Cummings poem. Yet most art historians agree with Guillaume Apollinaire, who said in 1912, in the *The Cubist Painters*—many of the artists were his personal friends—that realism was the movement's goal and Courbet, its father.

Even the pictorial distortion that continues to distress many people reflects a realistic impulse. As Gertrude Stein said of

Pablo Picasso, the artist's greatest struggle was to find a way to represent what he saw—what he actually saw, that is, rather than a combination of what he saw *and* what he remembered and thought. Thus, if he saw only one eye of a model, only one eye existed for him as a painter and only one eye appeared on his canvas.

In America, one of the leaders of the realist movement was Robert Henri. As teacher and as friend Henri had an immense impact on his contemporaries. Inspired by Emerson and Whitman and, later, by the example of Theodore Dreiser, Henri urged artists to follow their individual bents, to put aside academic finish and technical facility, to forget the rules of design, to escape the merely pretty in subject matter and treatment, and to recover instead a fresh and direct vision of the truth of things.

The realist movement for which Henri was one major spokesman produced a new atmosphere in American art. Like most self-styled revolutionists the realist knew much more certainly what he opposed than what he favored. But, in loose and largely unexamined form, he built on one fundamental, positive premise about the nature of art. He believed that nature itself was art. His attack on the turn-of-the-century tastemakers' canons of good taste aimed ultimately at a recovery of raw, often crude, but basically beautiful nature—not what man had traditionally thought nature was, but what nature was in and of itself.

Whitman stood as authority for this view. *Leaves of Grass,* Whitman had claimed, was not so much a work of art; it was nature itself speaking "without check, with original energy." These United States are themselves the great poem, he had said on another occasion; and his catalogues of place names, occupations, sounds, smells, and activities were his effort to transfer life directly to the printed page. John Sloan witnessed to the leavening effect of this emphasis. "Henri was my father in Art," he said in 1948. "I got Whitman through him. Whitman's love for all men, his beautiful attitude toward the physical, the absence of prudishness–. . . all this represented a force for freedom. . . . I liked what resulted from his catalogues of life. They helped to interest me in the details of life around me."[14]

The same excitement informed E. E. Cummings' response to the paintings of Picasso. Picasso viewed the world from such a fresh and personal perspective that he in effect liberated the actual world from the merely real world to which centuries of conventionality had consigned it. A poetic tribute which voices Cummings' esthetic at least as much as it does Picasso's begins:

> Picasso
> you give us Things
> which
> bulge. . .

> [*Poems 1923-1954*, p. 144]

As the poem develops it is clear that Cummings found in Picasso great restorative powers. His paintings revealed the dynamic qualities of the material world. They treated the spaces between objects with as much care as the objects themselves. Indeed, they often made "dead space" solid and alive, thus restoring a tangible significance to an aspect of actuality which the conventional purposes of man and the conventional techniques of painters ignored.

The Picasso paintings which Cummings saw in the Museum of Western Art remained one of the few pleasing experiences on his whole trip to Russia, as he recounted them in *Eimi*. In an atmosphere totally dominated by the dead abstractions approved by Communist officialdom ("incredible apotheosis of isn't"), the paintings were an acute contrast: "Beautiful, beyond wonder, murderings of reality."

But Communist Russia of the 1930's was, for Cummings, merely an extreme case of a sickness which pervaded modern civilization. Modern man desperately needed artists to save him from his commitment to material ease, a commitment so unanimous and so total that a whole society had come, as it were, to look on the world with a single pair of eyes or, as Cummings has frequently put it, everyone had become everyone else. To meet the need, however, art itself had to reform. It had to recover the capacity to see nature itself as the greatest work of art. His sense of nature as art is the reason why Cummings was so moved once by the ironic accident of a nude woman standing "framed" by the window of a room. The "picture" that resulted was far better than anything that could have been composed by mere human genius. And the same Ultimate Artist who composes nudes also paints astronomically on the night sky:

> night's speechless carnival
> the painting
> of the dark
> with meteors
>
> [*Poems 1923-1954*, p. 31]

IV *The Cult of the Ugly*

One important concomitant of Cummings' faith in nature as the most perfect art was his cultivation of the ugly in his work. On his Russian trip, Cummings visited a "Very Bad Childs" restaurant, one among many unsatisfactory experiences. This one was partly redeemed, however, by his meeting there "a truly magnificent stink."[15] The incident, humorous to be sure, reflects at the same time a very fundamental component of his esthetic.

The use of "junk materials" in the painting and sculpture of the post-World War II era has produced shock and disgust. There is a strong temptation to dismiss an artist's use of charred wood, canvas with holes in it, rusty machinery, bent nails, burnt paint, and old newspapers. Before doing so, however, we must at least acknowledge how large a part of the art of the last hundred years may be gone before we can find a convenient stopping point. A line so direct that it almost seems an umbilical cord connects Pollock's painting and David Smith's sculpture of the 1950's with the Dada movement of the World War I period. The junk materials used in the visual arts parallel precisely poems like Allen Ginsberg's "Sunflower Sutra" with its discovery of a single sunflower amid dockside debris. The following quotation from a book review in *The New Republic* bespeaks a whole era. "I feel," the reviewer said:

> as if I had been rooting long, desperate hours in a junk heap, irritably but thoroughly pawing over all sorts of queer, nameless garbage, rotting tin cans, owls' skeletons, the poisonous fragments of human apparatus rusting into morbid greens, yellows, oranges, and yet as if prodding about among these and other objects best touched only with a stick, I had come away at last with some lumps of curious, discolored but none the less precious metal.

The review, entitled "Garbage and Gold," might have concerned

the Beat Generation of the 1950's. In fact, it appeared on May
10, 1922; the book was E. E. Cummings' *The Enormous Room.*
But the cult of the ugly extends even further back in time. It
includes the "ash can" painters, Stephen Crane's *Maggie: A Girl
of the Streets,* and the famous line in Whitman's "Song of Myself"
which asserts that "the scent of these arm-pits aroma [is] finer
than prayer." And it extends as well into the insistent dissonance
of contemporary music and even into Frank Lloyd Wright's use
of pre-cast concrete blocks in the Millard House. The basic
impulse in this insistence on ugliness is the realist's belief that
the beauty of nature depends, in some sense, on its coexistence
with ugliness and, therefore, that beauty in art is not worth much
unless it also acknowledges the ugly. As Cummings says in
"Jehovah buried, Satan dead," the world has lost something very
important with "badness not being felt as bad" [*Poems 1923-
1954,* p. 314]. To achieve beauty, twentieth-century realism seems
to say, the artist needs boldly to dare its opposite and, if possible,
arrange a convincing, difficult, last-minute rescue.

Ugliness appears in Cummings' poetry in many different ways.
It appears in the choice of such subject matter as the smell of
manure or the loveless old crones in #35 of *95 Poems,* each of
whom insists upon her own virtue and the other's corruption. It
appears also in the accents, language, and attitudes of people
whose speech becomes the very fabric of a poem like "oil tel duh
woil doi sez" [*Poems 1923-1954,* p. 224].

One of the best of Cummings' "ugly" poems concerns a drunk
throwing up in the men's room of a restaurant. It renders fully
the details of the incident, and it succeeds remarkably well,
finally, in stealing gold from amidst the garbage:

a) glazed mind layed in a
                              urinal
howlessly and without why
(quite minus gal or
                              pal

slightly too sick to rightly die)
"gedup"
            the gentscoon coos
gently:tug?g(ing intently it

```
                refuses.
                        to refuse;
                just,look)ing dead but not complete
                -ly not(not as look men

                who are turned to seem)
                                        "stetti"
                and
                        willbeishfully bursting un-
                eats wasvino isspaghett(i
                                [Poems 1923-1954, p. 280]
```

The drunk's almost complete passivity is implicit in his standing before the urinal, staring "howlessly and without why," that
is, without appearing to ask either how? or why? In his dissocia-
tion he has no sense of himself, no sense of personal dignity
that needs protecting. In response to the attendant's solicitude
(the question mark in the middle of "tugging" suggests the
gentleness of his action), the drunk continues to "ing intently."
He continues, that is, to engage in an action without content, or
to do nothing. By contrast to both the passive drunk and the
solicitous attendant, Cummings says, the other men in the room
are aloof and self-possessed and therefore completely dead as
human beings.

At the very end of the poem the drunk comes to the utter
extremity of his helplessness as he throws up his spaghetti dinner.
Cummings treats this climax with a touch of humor, but he is
essentially serious when he points to the vomiting man, and says,
here is "a . . . i". Men who insulate themselves from what they
take to be ugly merely "seem" to be men. The only real man is
the one who can surrender himself to the world as given.

The drunk, confessing the nausea in his stomach, is an image
of the artist confessing the ugliness in his world. Basically, the
artist of the ugly says that the world is more beautiful and more
harmonious than mankind has generally realized. In so doing,
he echoes Thoreau's famous comment toward the end of *Walden*
about the dead horse. The horse lying in a hollow by the path
to his house:

> compelled me sometimes to go out of my way, especially
> in the night when the air was heavy, but the assurance it

gave me of the strong appetite and inviolable health of Nature was my compensation for this. I love to see that Nature is so rife with life that myriads can be afforded to be sacrificed and suffered to prey on one another. . . . The impression made on a wise man is that of universal innocence. Poison is not poisonous after all, nor are any wounds fatal.

V *The Necessity of Fragmentation*

The cult of ugliness is one dimension of the realist's faith in nature as the ultimate art. Another is the rejection of some of the more fully accepted methods of treating nature in art and the search for new ways of coming closer to nature's essence. In the catalogue for the Rochester show of his painting, Cummings commented on representationalism in painting. The total impression he created was that he was not very much interested in the subject. Casually, he said of himself: "I am a painter, and painting is non-representational."[16]

Elsewhere he took note of varying artistic fashions and observed that once his painting was regarded as not adequately representational whereas by 1954 it was not adequately non-representational. His summation: "And your stupid wiseguy doing his worst to deny Nature equals your clever fool who did his best to possess Her."[17] Despite Cummings' sense that non-representational art is not a worthy subject for discussion, it is important to see how deeply he responded to both its ends and means.

His general position is implicit in his reference to Picasso's "beautiful, beyond wonder, murderings of reality." "Reality" needs to be murdered because it is so much a compound of conventional ways of seeing that men cannot see Reality. And, like Picasso and many other artists since the Impressionists, Cummings, too, searched persistently for significant techniques of fragmentation and recombination. He broke off lines in the middle of words; placed the first syllable of a word at the beginning of a poem and the last at the end; strewed capital letters about with abandon; used verbs, adverbs, and adjectives as though they were nouns; used nouns as though they were verbs. His variations and the effects achieved are too numerous for cataloguing here.[18] In one way or another, however, they force the reader to a more immediate awareness of reality than would otherwise be possible. In a sense, most of Cummings' strange devices enable the reader to hear trains "chewing." They fracture the reader's expectations about the meaning of words and their relationship to one another so that he may see what the world is really like.

Most people, artists and non-artists alike, believe that clarity of expression demands the correct words in correct sequence. Thus: "Her hand felt soft when it touched me." But modern painters in their rejection of vanishing point perspective say, with Cummings, that ordinary 'correctness' simply will not do the job. If the artist would communicate what the touch of her hand really felt like, he must somehow break up traditional logical categories which, while they organize thought, inhibit perception. In this situation Cummings once broke up the word "soft" and wrote it:

> so
> !f!
> t . . .
>
> [*Poems 1923-1954*, p. 458]

By isolating the "so" of "soft," he added a "logical" intensification by suggesting the idea "so soft." More importantly, the exclamation points surrounding the "f" make the sound of the letter a metaphor for his precise meaning. Cummings says to us, "If you really want to know what I mean by 'soft,' then listen intently, even feel the letter 'f.' Say it to yourself and observe the way you blow air over your lips. That's my meaning!"

But there is more involved in Cummings' techniques of fragmentation than the desire to improve on the art of the past. Not only did Cummings aim to be more effectively realistic than earlier realists, not only did he wish to be more faithful to nature than earlier generations; he wanted also to render a reality which had itself changed. The twentieth century has witnessed revolutionary discoveries about the nature of the world, with respect to both interstellar space and microcosmic, atomic space.

Even schoolchildren today know that we need microscopes and telescopes in order really to see what's going on in the physical world. They realize that ordinary eyesight, hearing, smelling, and touching are too imprecise for certain kinds of observation. But the most revolutionary discovery of modern science is that the physical world is—in the present state of our knowledge—not only extremely difficult to observe but *theoretically unobservable*.

Radar can measure the position of an airplane far beyond the reach of the human eye aided even by the most high-powered telescope. It does so by bouncing short radio waves off the airplane and by recording the echoes. Submicroscopic measurements are made similarly with X-rays or very high frequency gamma rays. But Heisenberg's principle of uncertainty posited that, if the atom to be located is small enough, the rays sent out by the measuring instrument will exert such a force on the atom that they will themselves dislocate what they are supposed to locate. Quantum physics is reduced, therefore, to dealing with large numbers of atoms in constant motion. Since it cannot even hope to observe an individual atom, it is forced to think in terms of what Sir James Jeans called a "statistical atom."

There is, of course, a strange paradox here. Using mathematical notations, modern science is capable of almost incredibly accurate definitions of the physical world, even though these are but highly precise predictions. At the same time, however, it acknowledges a theoretically impassable gulf between its calculations and the objective world of essentially unobservable phenomena. As one commentator has put it, the scientist is today "in the position of a blind man trying to discern the shape and texture of a snowflake. As soon as it touches his fingers or his tongue it dissolves." The only absolute surety he has left is motion itself.

VI *The World As Motion*

E. E. Cummings has expressed nothing but contempt for the scientific enterprise of abstraction and prediction. And yet his labor has clearly been, in part, to find artistic embodiments of the world of motion revealed so strikingly by modern science. Other influences were at work, to be sure. Not the least of them is the visible motion that characterizes the twentieth century— cars and airplanes, jack-hammers, a vastly increased population. But one of the few specific esthetic intentions to which Cummings has ever been willing to admit is the creation of movement. And in this concern he again typifies the art of a century. When John Marin was asked to explain his dissatisfaction with his student days at the Pennsylvania Academy for Fine Arts, he said that a student there "paints a boat so it looks like a boat. But what has he got? The boat doesn't *do* anything. It doesn't move in the water, it is blown by no tempest. . . Art must show what goes on in the world."[19]

Faced with a similar question, Cummings wrote the following for the Foreword of *Is 5:*

> On the assumption that my technique is either complicated or original or both, the publishers have politely requested me to write an introduction to this book.
>
> At least my theory of technique, if I have one, is very far from original; nor is it complicated. I can express it in fifteen words, by quoting The Eternal Question And Immortal Answer of burlesk, viz. "Would you hit a woman with a child?—No, I'd hit her with a brick." Like the burlesk comedian, I am abnormally fond of that precision which creates movement.

The meaning of realism is, in part, then a sense of the world as motion. Motion is both an esthetic principle and a central theme in Cummings' art. It even characterizes his signature, which he once described as "making rollercoastering from C an arching skid into gs."

VII ‑ *Two Bird Poems*

Cummings' realist esthetics can, perhaps, best be summarized through a comparison of one of his bird poems with William Cullen Bryant's "To a Waterfowl." Bryant's poem, written in 1815, opens:

> Whither, midst falling dew,
> While glow the heavens with the last steps of day,
> Far, through their rosy depths, dost thou pursue
> Thy solitary way?

The last stanza reads

He who, from zone to zone,
Guides through the boundless sky thy certain flight,
In the long way that I must tread alone,
Will lead my steps aright.

The fundamental experience of Bryant's poem is his observation of the waterfowl flying slowly and steadily across the evening sky, and finally disappearing. He meditates upon this vision and concludes with the affirmation that God will direct him as He seems to direct the bird. The strategic problem at the heart of the poem is to present the perception of the bird in such a way as to persuade the reader that the bird's flight is purposeful and that the purpose is God's purpose.

The second stanza is Bryant's most successful effort. Throughout most of the poem, Bryant proceeds indirectly by trying to make his own voice persuasive. In the second stanza, however, he suggests a clear visual image:

Vainly the fowler's eye
Might mark thy distant flight to do thee wrong,
As, darkly seen against the crimson sky,
Thy figure floats along.

The stanza asks that we consider the way a distant bird looks when viewed through the sight of a gun. The peculiar sense of distance that results—somewhat like looking through the wrong end of a telescope—goes a long way toward inducing the reader to participate in the experience of the poem as a whole.

From the perspective of a Cummings admirer, however, even this image is largely intellectual. Bryant does not, in any literal way, show what a bird looks like through a gunsight; he merely asks that we consider what a hypothetical fowler might see. (One can almost imagine Cummings arranging an oversized, capital *O* with a period inside and, perhaps a line of dashes to indicate the horizon line.)

Cummings' poem #46 from *No Thanks* [*Poems 1923-1954*, p. 307] is very like Bryant's. It too places a bird against a round object. Where Bryant asks us to hold a moving bird in a gunsight, however, Cummings shows us a bird crossing in front of the sun:

swi(
     across!gold's

rouNdly
)ftblac
kl(ness)y

a-motion-upo-nmotio-n

Less?
     thE
(against
is
)Swi

mming

(w-a)s
bIr

d,

The fundamental experience of this poem is the wonderful suddenness of a bird's flight across the sun, the poet's subsequent struggle to realize and name what he sees, and his tentative judgment that the initial response was more valuable than the final realization. The problem at the heart of the poem is to present the perception of the bird in such a way as to persuade the reader that a significant distinction exists between perception and conception.

The poet's first impression is simply of the speed of an unidentified object's flight. But before he has even enunciated his first word, he realizes that he must qualify. He has perceived not the speed of a single object but rather the speedy passage of one object before another. The sense of speed is communicated by the suddenness of the parenthetical interruption; by the lack of clear syntactical relationships (suggesting, perhaps, the stutter of a man moved to speech before he clearly knows what he wants to say); and by the severely limited language which refers to the most primary qualities only: to speed, direction, color, and shape.

"a-motion-upo-nmotio-n/Less?" begins the speaker's effort to recapture, to understand, to think about what he is seeing and to estimate its value. The first of the two lines is the longest line in the poem, and the letters are arranged in a symmetrical pattern. These qualities of the line itself may suggest the peculiarly impressive qualities of the experience. The question posed by the two lines together confirms that the speaker's sense of his experience is that, in its striking speed, it has the quality of stasis, as though for a single instant the world is standing still. The isolation "Less" suggests that the speaker knows both objects are moving and yet, wonderfully, he senses that at least one of the objects is still. If the hyphens mean that "a-motion-upo-nmotio-n" is a single word, then the sensation that puzzles him is, to borrow mathematical language, motionlessness-squared.

Line eight, the middle line of the poem, marks the speaker's first effort to construct a whole sentence, a whole thought about his experience. In two sharp contrasts Cummings indicates, that in his judgment, this conceptualizing process tends to censor the vitality of life. "Against" contrasts with "across" and suggests the speaker's compulsion to freeze the action in order to talk about it. "Swi/mming" contrasts with "swi/ft" and suggests that the conscious intellect is unable to sustain the paradox of a speed which is motionless, and is forced to substitute instead a mathematical average of the two, namely the slow movement of swimming.

By the time the intellect has really begun to take charge, however, the experience itself is already past history and, with the naming finally of the first object to catch his attention, the poet seems simply to lose interest and give up. To continue the effort to organize the experience would be merely to murder what is already dead.

Cummings' use of capital letters in this poem is puzzling, as it frequently is elsewhere.[20] The development of the poem as a whole, however, suggests a tentative comment about the capital "I" in "bIrd." If the process of conceptualization is a movement away from the complexity of life, Cummings may be saying that it is also a movement toward the self, toward man's self-conscious desire to understand and control the world. Whether or not this is a legitimate interpretation, the identification of rational thought and egoism is certainly true to the spirit of Cummings' ideas in general and to the deepest meaning of his esthetic realism in particular. For his ideas about art are ultimately religious, just as his ideas about man and society are.

Bryant's poem about the waterfowl moves from the image of a bird to an *idea* about the poet's own relation to God. Cummings' poem moves in the same direction. But, whereas Bryant takes hope from the process, Cummings does not. Indeed, Cummings' poem is finally a parable illustrating what, in *i. Six Nonlectures,* he called "the satanic rape of matter by mind." The function of art is to take man beyond the confines of his own mind and to put him in touch with "whatever is hair-raising, breath-taking and pore-opening." Art must always stem from a "vast and painful process of unthinking." It is, after all, "a question of being alive."

CHAPTER 5

The Esthetics of Formalism

"Art, as I say and resay, is composition."
—Leo Stein

"For those who can feel the significance of form, art
can never be less than a religion."
—Clive Bell

IN RADICALLY condensed form, Cummings expressed his
realist esthetic in his definition of a poet as "a somebody who
sees a thing in its magnificent particularity." There is a kind of
muscularity in this position. It suggests a man who resolutely
uses his own eyes, who will not be influenced by anyone else,
and who takes nothing for granted. He doesn't worry about the
frills of expression, about technique or form. What's really important is to *see*, and if things are seen with sufficient depth and
clarity the reader will see them too.

I *The Traditions of Poe and Whistler*

But there is another side to Cummings' esthetics, just as there
is another side to the esthetics of his entire generation. They
were all formalists. To borrow Marianne Moore's phrase, they
all believed in "imaginary gardens with real toads in them."
They believed that the reality of poetic toads depends on their
relation to an artistic structure as well as to actual toads that
might have been hopping about outside Miss Moore's window.
How well toads and gardens work together is at least as important as what they are separately. The artist is a coach whose job
is to bring out the best in his material and to coax it into func-
tioning as a unit.

To appreciate the formalist aspect of Cummings' esthetics, we must again see the development of his thinking against the background of contemporary art in general, and of painting in particular; literary history alone will not suffice. For reasons which have as much to do with the accidents of history as with logic, formalism has been an important presence in modern literature and yet never so bluntly articulated as in painting. From James McNeill Whistler to the present, important painters and critics have repeatedly taken the extreme formalist position that painting is wholly a matter of what happens on the surface of the canvas and has nothing whatever to do with the actuality of landscapes or nudes or potted flowers. From Edgar Allan Poe to the present, writers and literary critics have frequently approached this position but no important figure ever reached the extreme.

In developing a position with which to challenge the undue moralism which Poe identified with literary New England, he stressed the constructive aspect of literature. The writer must first conceive "a single effect." Then from the first to the last, every sentence must contribute to this effect: "In the whole composition there should be no word written of which the tendency, direct or indirect, is not to the one pre-established design." Art, Poe said, is the creation of such designs. It is not moral instruction, it is not the expression of Truth. But Truth returned by a side door in Poe's thinking, as it was later to do in several generations of writers, both American and European, who looked to him as their esthetic father.

When Poe sought to elaborate the idea of "single effect," he explained that he sought the special quality of music which is, he thought, the suggestive indefiniteness of vague and therefore of spiritual effect.[1] The doctrine of vagueness implicitly acknowledges that art must refer to the world beyond itself even while its intent is to hold the world at a distance. Baudelaire, who introduced Poe to the French symbolist poets, responded to Poe's conception of the poet as a disciplined craftsman and to his musical analogy, but he also accepted the confusing idea of art's suggestive indefiniteness. The very name "symbolist" points to the realistic or referential dimension of meaning; and much of the confusion about modern poetry has come directly from the readers' difficulty in determining what the poetry refers to. The oft-repeated explanation that a symbol is a metaphor with one term missing compounds the confusion rather than clarifying it. Despite the effort to focus literature's attention on formal problems, therefore, the Poe tradition has, in subtle ways, held the door open for realism.

The history of the esthetics of painting took a parallel, yet significantly different, course; and this was the tradition which influenced E. E. Cummings. To some degree, Whistler was motivated, as Poe had been, by the desire to escape the imposition of moral demands on art. He objected, for example, to the notion that a work of art was noble if it had a noble subject matter. But, in developing his philosophy, he hit upon a crucially important metaphor. In his famous "Ten O'Clock Lecture," he attacked the people who looked "not *at* a picture, but *through* it, at some human fact, that shall, or shall not, from a social point of view, better their mental or moral state." The metaphor, suggestive of the difference between a wall and a window, went beyond the immediate needs of the argument. Realism, after all, also fought a battle against excess moralism. Its great hope was to break out of the confines of traditional ideas of the good, the true, and the beautiful and into the world as it really is. But realism believed in nature; Whistler did not. The idea that painting was to be looked at, rather than through, had profound implications; and Whistler was aware of them, and he asserted them vigorously.

When England's leading art critic John Ruskin denounced Whistler for his "Cockney impudence" in "flinging a pot of paint in the public's face," Whistler replied with a series of articles in the press and a famous law suit. The overwhelming majority of the people, he said, were incapable of considering a painting simply as a painting; they were wedded to the idea of looking for a recognizable scene or story. But the majority was mistaken. A painting, Whistler said, is basically an organization of colors and shapes just as a Beethoven sonata is an organization of chords. To underline the musical analogy, he had called many of his own paintings arrangements, harmonies, and nocturnes. Referring to his best known, single painting, he said:

> Take the picture of my mother, exhibited at the Royal Academy as an 'Arrangement in Grey and Black.' Now that is what it is. To me it is interesting as a picture of my

mother; but what can or ought the public to care about the identity of the portrait?

The imitator is a poor kind of creature. If the man who paints only the tree, or flower, or other surface he sees before him were an artist, the king of artists would be the photographer. It is for the artist to do something beyond this: in portrait painting to put on canvas something more than the face the model wears for that one day; to paint the man, in short, as well as his features; in arrangement of colours to treat a flower as his key, not as his model.[2]

It is interesting that Whistler should have emphasized the analogy to music just as Poe did. He was followed in this usage by almost every painter of note up to the present. But the painters did not mean quite the same thing when they referred to music as the writers in the Poe tradition did. They were not talking about the suggestively indefinite relation of their work to reality; they were talking rather about their work as a structure of surface relationships which existed on a plane entirely different from reality. Nature, Whistler admitted, contained the elements of pictures—colors and forms. But artists are responsible for selecting the elements and ordering them and creating beauty. Nature is chaos; only artists create harmony. "To say to the painter that Nature is to be taken as she is," Whistler said, "is to say to the player, that he may sit on the piano." Failing to anticipate the day when pianists would play tone clusters by striking the piano with the entire forearm, Whistler reasoned that, while nature provided all the notes of the piano keyboard, music depended upon human composition. Far from being always right artistically, "Nature is usually wrong," he concluded. Rare indeed is the occasion when nature produces the perfection which art demands.

By the twentieth century, Whistler's emphasis on the artist's creating his own harmony rather than imitating nature's had become a commonplace among the post-impressionist painters and their critical supporters. More articulately—because more extreme—than in comparable expressions by writers, painters said repeatedly that they were far from trying to establish significant relationships with reality; on the contrary, their work stood over against reality. Cezanne had rejected the precise observation of the impressionists because nature is a "chaos of disorganized movement"; art required, therefore, a reorganization of nature rather than mere passive sense perception, however precise. Matisse had insisted on his right to use color freely, without regard for its representational quality, because the ultimate expressive value of painting resides in "a complete accord of living colors, a harmony analogous to that of musical composition." And the story was widespread about the woman who visited Matisse's studio one day and commented that an unfinished work, still sitting on the painter's easel, had represented a woman with a disproportionately long arm. "Madam, you are mistaken," Matisse is said to have replied. "This is not a woman. This is a picture."

By the time Cummings began to formulate his esthetic, a new vocabulary had grown up so that even the literate public could begin to talk knowingly about formalist art; and, within a few years, this vocabulary had reached the level of the "How to See Modern Pictures" books. The terms "abstract" and "non-representational," interestingly enough, point to the referential aspect of art; but they do so negatively, like Poe's idea of vagueness. Meanwhile, however, art was being widely spoken of also as "design," as "composition," and as various kinds of "form"—"plastic form," "architectural form," "ultimate form," and "significant form," none of which had counterparts in literature.[3]

Clive Bell's idea of significant form was the most influential. Without exaggeration it could be said that, if Whistler was formalism's spiritual father, Bell was its chief prophet. In art, Bell said, "the chatter and tumult of material existence is unheard." Rather, the life of a work of art is a matter of formal, internal relations. In a work that has significant form, everything reduces to the relations among its colors and lines. Far from concluding, however, that the artist's stature was in any way lessened by his imprisonment in his own methods and materials, Bell insisted that the artist is at least the equal of the priest. For precisely in escaping the restraints of public facts and ideas, the artist provides insight into the ultimate nature of things. "For those who can feel the significance of form," he said, "art can never be less than a religion."[4] The esthetics of formalism had arrived, clearly stated and restated by painters and critics of painting from Whistler's time, and suffusing the art world in general.

II *The Artist As Professional*

In the light of this background, Cummings' graduation address on "The New Art" becomes a peculiarly interesting document, as much for its imperfections as for its merits. It is remarkable that, as a college senior in 1915, he should have been alive to the principles of formalism. It is even more remarkable that his analysis reflected precisely the status of those principles in the contemporary art world, for he had difficulty in trying to apply formalist principles to poetry, and this difficulty accurately reflected the greater clarity with which the visual arts had developed the principles than had literature.

Cummings set out "to sketch briefly the parallel developments of the New Art in painting, sculpture, music, and literature." His central thesis was that order and coherence existed where the public and the critics found only incoherence and abnormality. He acknowledged that serious critics had already learned to accept Cezanne and Matisse by 1915, but beyond them, he said, "contemporary criticism becomes, for the most part, rampant abuse, and . . . prejudice utters its storm of condemnation. I refer to that peculiar phase of modern art called indiscriminately, 'Cubism,' and 'Futurism.'" Cummings' explanation for the furor was that recent painters and sculptors were basing their work on a new approach. Their primary concerns were the fundamental properties of the material of their art and their organization. The Cubists' distinguishing trait was that they "use design to express their personal reaction to the subject" and that they "take this design from geometry." "By using an edge in place of a curve," he added, "a unique tactual value is obtained." And later he referred to Brancusi's "Mlle. Pogany" as "the triumph of line for line's sake over realism."

Whether or not his decision to talk about the visual arts first and literature last is significant, it certainly is significant that, when he came to the last section, his speech degenerated into some incoherence; and, in talking about Gertrude Stein, he was not even sure he was still talking about art. "Gertrude Stein," he said, "subordinates the meaning of words to the beauty of words themselves. Her art is the logic of literary sound painting carried to its extreme." But when he asked himself whether, despite the logic, Stein's poetry was art, his answer was only that it was original exploration that warranted sympathetic attention. Cummings, then, at this early stage in his career, obviously felt more at home in thinking about the visual arts than about literature.[5] It is not surprising, therefore, that he should have continued to range widely for esthetic experiences with which to refine his thought.

The realist dimension of Cummings' esthetics suggests the mindless primitivist that many critics have taken him for. His insistence on the naïveté of children and his strictures against thought and, even, art have encouraged this view of him. In one sense, therefore, he merits, along with Mark Twain, Matthew Arnold's sobriquet—the divine amateur. But Cummings was also a professional. He took a professional's attitude toward art. He admired professional work, he studied it, and he worked for it himself. This was the formalist side of him, the side that values technique over subject matter and the nature of artistic materials and organization over clear vision.

Indeed, Cummings' criticism often surprises even those who are generally familiar with it; for, in the midst of a highly romantic passage of praise for a writer or painter, he will say that the artist's striking success reflects his mastery of his craft. In a 1920 essay about T. S. Eliot's first two volumes of poetry, for example, Cummings compared Eliot favorably with Cezanne and Gaston Lachaise and then said (in recognizable Cummingsese) that Eliot makes his readers come alive. But it was Eliot's overwhelming sense of technique that Cummings so much admired, not his movingly perceptive representation of modern life. What most moved Cummings was Eliot's precise vocabulary and his "extraordinarily tight orchestration of the shapes of sounds."[6]

This reaction to Eliot was typical of Cummings. Art was always, for him, as for the entire Whistler tradition, far more than an emotional response to life. He often talked as though an artist needed no more than a pure heart and a pure soul, but it is important to see how thoroughly he also recognized the roles of intelligence and skill and hard work. If at times he talked as though all art were one art, he was also sensitive to the techniques which were peculiar to each. When he attended the theater, for example, he was acutely conscious of such dramaturgical problems as the treatment of upstage areas which, in the hands of unskilled directors, ordinarily become mere excess, dead space. Early in his visit to Moscow when Cummings attended a bad, melodramatic, Russian propaganda play, he, nevertheless, found some moving moments, because he was so completely alive to the special techniques of the theater. Cummings revealingly described the experience in *Eimi*:

> now here's tay-ahter—sense of pretend,promising nonsense of actuality. Dissonant pipings "set the key": stark exposition(Yank-Chink dialogue)maekr are removed by chorus, opening stage which is promptly animated by the crossing of a tiny boat(water,real)and which subsequently is annihilated by the(waterless)movingup of the Chief Object, i.e. battleship,toward audience;abstract use of noisesound to invent space(distance)and place(location);nouns arbitrarily are represented by merely wheres,e.g.sailors face X and look—X being a plane or anything whatever or nothing, being not looked At,being unimportant with respect to looking which itself constitutes its target
>
> and from these promisings am happy. For I taste technique:smell style;touch something(not definably,particularly, logically which seems)thoroughly which Is: . . .[7]

From Cummings' description, it does not sound as though the Moscow director had displayed any peculiar genius in stagecraft. To suggest the presence of an airplane by an appropriate stare into the wings is conventional enough. What is striking about Cummings' report is what it reveals about Cummings' own awareness of the smallest detail of technique for its own sake.

And, of course, he brought this sensitivity with him to his favorite medium, the revue. In 1926 he analyzed the essential structural device of the Parisian revue for *Vanity Fair*. "By the laws of its own structure, which are the irrevocable laws of juxtaposition and contrast," he said, "the revue is a use of everything trivial or plural to intensify what is singular and fundamental. In the case of the Folies-Bergere, the revue is the use of ideas, smells, colours, Irving Berlin, nudes, tactility, collapsible stairs, three dimensions and fireworks to intensify Mlle. Josephine Baker."[8]

Just one year before, for the same magazine, Cummings had written a similar, and even more interesting, piece about American burlesque. In a long introduction he commented on the nature of art and some of the important differences among particular art forms. He contrasted, for example, the static nature of painting and sculpture with the time dimension of music, literature—and burlesque. Then he described, by way of illustration, a famous routine of comedian Jack Shargel's, a routine which had given Cummings (he said) one of his most extraordinary experiences, a complete esthetic emotion. Shargel, a very Semitic-looking, black derbied, ill-clothed clown, walks onstage. An enormous woman hands him a red rose. Shargel smells it with grandiloquent gestures, and then exquisitely wafts it through the air. The rose floats to the floor and lands to the accompaniment of a loud crash. Cummings' explanation of why he was moved by the Shargel routine is illuminating. The release, he said, of all the unrose qualities in the world enhances the essence of rose.[9]

It is difficult to know how seriously to take some of Cummings' judgments about the esthetic value of burlesque, particularly when he claimed to have been more enthralled by Jack Shargel than by Cezanne. One thing is clear, however. He knew the difference between art and life, and he knew, as he once said of the sculpture of Lachaise, that the naïve artlessness which he admired so much is, in actuality, one of the highest achievements of art—skilled, trained, calculated, intelligent.

III   The Meanings of Language

Clearly, painting and sculpture were major influences on Cummings' poetry as well as his esthetics. Cummings' critics have called attention before to the poet's relation to contemporary painting. They have, however, vastly underestimated the depth of this relation. What Cummings learned from his study of the visual arts went far beyond his interest in poetry's visual appearance. Certainly, it went beyond the fact that certain poems visually represent objects, such as a wine glass or the smoke from a locomotive. John Peale Bishop, the most perceptive of those who have commented on the relationship between Cummings and modern painters, has said that Cummings "juxtaposes words as they do pigments."[10]

But even this statement points to a mere detail. The visual arts taught Cummings, primarily, to think about poetry as a structure of interrelated parts, appearing on the page of a book. While the leading spirits of American poetry in the second decade were working for clear, concrete images and for the accents of the spoken language, Cummings was beginning to develop an attitude toward language which paralleled the attitudes of contemporary painters and sculptors. He had said of Brancusi that he seduced the human form into a sensual geometry. The point was that Brancusi had created an esthetic composition by manipulating bronze into a unity of curved lines and surfaces. He admired Lachaise for his brilliant handling of stone. Not only did Cummings treat poetry as a two-dimensional canvas, therefore, but he also investigated the full plastic possibilities of language itself.

Spoken language offers many different qualities for poetic exploitation. The most common dimension is the conceptual or semantic or, to borrow a term from the previous discussion, the referential. Words, that is, point beyond themselves to ideas, to events, to things in human experience. Poets, in particular, have been aware of three additional dimensions of language: the aural, the accentual, and the temporal. These three are the traditional elements of versification: the sounds of vowels and consonants, the relative emphasis required by the different syllables of words, and the time required to enunciate a word or a line.[11]

Recent linguistic study has sharpened awareness of a fourth dimension. Some words and phrases do not so much *mean* as *function*. Words like "the," "and," "which," and "it" serve primarily to indicate relationships among other words and phrases rather than to denote or point to the world beyond. To these four dimensions Cummings has added a fifth: language's visual appearance. But Cummings' real contribution has not been merely the addition of the visual element but rather the imaginative exploitation of all the basic properties of language.

Cummings has been severely taken to task for his failure to be more interested in the conceptual aspect of words. The most important critique of this sort was R. P. Blackmur's "Notes on E. E. Cummings' Language" in 1930. Blackmur objected to Cummings' reliance on abstract words like "flower" and insisted that the full meaning of such words remained locked in Cummings' own personal experience instead of being communicated through the medium of the printed page.[12] In Blackmur's view, that is, a reader must know whether the poet means a red carnation in the buttonhole of an usher at a June wedding, a shriveled gardenia crushed in the pages of a schoolgirl's diary, or a single cactus bloom in the Arizona desert.

But this is to insist exclusively upon the referential in art and to miss the import of Cummings' formalism, for Cummings was interested in the wholeness of language and in the full range of its possibilities rather than in its limited, conceptual nature. And this interest produced Cummings' most distinctive single trait: his attention not only to words and sentences but also to parts of words and sentences, to syllables, parts of syllables, and even to individual letters and punctuation marks. He searched the smallest details of language in all its dimensions in his effort to extend the ways in which language could be used to communicate.

The stanza from "what if a much of a which of a wind," which has already been quoted in another connection, provides an interesting illustration of Cummings' special concern in poetry:

what if a much of a which of a wind
gives the truth to summer's lie;
bloodies with dizzying leaves the sun
and yanks immortal stars awry?
Blow king to beggar and queen to seem
(blow friend to fiend: blow space to time)
—when skies are hanged and oceans drowned,
the single secret will still be man
                    [*Poems 1923-1954*, p. 401]

For the most part these lines can be easily understood as conventional hyperbole—playfully exaggerated but fundamentally representational. "King" and "beggar" make a simple, conceptual opposition. The relation between "queen" and "seem" is more complicated. A conceptual opposition is enhanced by sound and by the use of a verb for a noun. The relation between "friend" and "fiend" is pure Cummings. The conceptual opposition remains, to be sure. But the primary interest in the phrase involves aural and visual aspects of language in addition to the conceptual. The meaning of the phrase does not depend at all, as Blackmur would have it, on the concreteness of the words. It does not depend primarily on their referential quality, although the presence of this quality is what prevents the phrase from being nonsense. Meaning here depends on what happens on the printed page itself. The wind is neither defined nor described; it is not referred to metaphorically. It acts. It blows the "r" out of "friend" and, in this simple move, turns it into its opposite. To say of Cummings that his meaning lies on the surface of his poems is not necessarily to render a legitimate objection to his art; it is, however, to describe one of the lessons that Cummings learned from formal developments in the visual arts of our time. This awareness of formal relationships permitted him to communicate with a new kind of dramatic immediacy.

Cummings' study of the properties of language also produced new ways of extending meaning. By breaking words into their component parts and recombining them, just as Cubism analyzed surfaces into planes and angles, Cummings developed uniquely vital ambiguities. Thus, at the climax of a poem about a sunrise, "itself" becomes "it:s;elf," and even as absolute an object as the risen sun has become "elfish" in its basic "self"—that is, a great, insubstantial mystery instead of a simple commonplace [*Poems 1923-1954*, p. 303].

The most notable instance of this plastic treatment of words was Cummings' use, in several poems, of the word "nowhere." In a poem on the death of critic Paul Rosenfeld, for example, he used the interior words: "no," "now," and "he." In addition, the "o" serves a rhyming function and also as a visual symbol of "the round little man we loved" [*Poems 1923-1954*, p. 433]. In the fourth poem of *95 Poems*, he emphasized only the two interior words "now" and "here"; but he did so with the most striking effectiveness, because in the plastic possibilities of this very abstract word he found the means to render the most central paradox in his entire understanding of life. The poem says:

this man's heart

. . .

. . . loves

nothing

as much as
how(first
the arri
-v-

in

-g)a snowflake twi-
sts
,on
its way to now

-here

The splitting of "nowhere" gathers the poem by asserting the ultimate identity of life and death. It says that annihilation, the disappearance of the snowflake into "nowhere," is the way to presence in this time and this place, "now" and "here." To induce belief in the identity of the opposites life and death, Cummings exploits the demonstrable linguistic truth that "now" + "here" = "nowhere."

Clearly, the dynamics of Cummings' treatment of "nowhere" involve an important conceptual or referential element. The word is peculiarly subject to plastic treatment because it does contain interior words with conceptual meanings of their own. There are nevertheless two important reasons for offering it to illustrate Cummings' formalism. The first is that no conceptual link ties together "now" and "nowhere." The link results purely from an accidental combination of letters. When, by contrast, Robert Frost says:

When the wind works against us in the dark,
And pelts with snow
The lower chamber window on the east,

he is exploiting two different, conceptual meanings of "pelt" in order to say that the snow both strikes the window and covers it with a protective skin. The second reason for citing the treatment of "nowhere" is the likelihood that Cummings did not discover its inherent ambiguity by puzzling over its meaning but rather by thinking about it as an object in itself, a structure of letters.

In effect, then, one of the major reasons for the strangeness of Cummings' poetry is that language itself is his principal metaphor. He demands of us that we inspect the printed page rather than look through it, that we seek for meaning in the arrangement of letters and words themselves before we ask what a poem represents. Cummings avoided the controversy that surrounded Whistler by leaving most of his poems untitled. We can easily imagine a poem like "nonsun blob" becoming a storm center, however. We can hear a critic crying out that Cummings has thrown an inkwell in the public's face. And then we can hear Cummings replying that his poem, "Portrait of the Growing World," is not really a portrait of anything, but rather an "Arrangement in Syntax and Diction."

The poet, Cummings said in the Foreword to *Is 5*, is "somebody who is obsessed by Making." The statement pointed to an important aspect of Cummings himself. He liked to enthrall people by constructing for them what they had never seen before. He liked to stretch his material. He often used punctuation and spacing to gain special effects from the temporal or the visual factor in language—to suggest, for example, through a kind of visual syncopation, the unevenness with which a curtain rises in a cheap nightclub. He often took one part of speech and placed it into a composition in such a way that it functioned like another, as in these lines (to which I have added italics):

> my father moved through dooms of love
> through *sames* of *am* through *haves* of *give*
>
> . . . .
> this motionless forgetful *where*
> turned at his glance to shining *here;*
>
> [*Poems 1923-1954*, p. 373]

As a contemporary painter might ambiguously have used a single curve for the neck of a vase and the edge of a guitar, Cummings often composed his syntax so that a single word both intensified a statement and raised a question about it, as the "how" does in "anyone lived in a pretty how town." Among other possibilities, however, "how" here also suggests that the townspeople are always asking how things work instead of simply accepting and enjoying them for what they are. The poet is a Maker, and he would like nothing better than to be told, as Cummings once said of Pablo Picasso, "you hew form truly" [*Poems 1923-1954*, p. 144].

IV *Conflicting Ideas and Esthetic Experience*

It is time, finally, to acknowledge that realism and formalism represent a flat contradiction in Cummings' esthetics. To recapitulate briefly: realism emphasizes that the world is ultimately harmonious and beautiful no matter how ugly or confusing it may seem; the function of the artist is to see through conventional representations of the world and present it as it really is, in order that artist and audience may see anew; the artist's fundamental talent is his capacity to see and respond to life with the utmost originality; and the work of art is therefore a peculiarly clear window onto the world beyond. Formalism, on the other hand, says that the world is chaotic; the function of the artist is to discover the full potentiality of his own materials and make of them a satisfyingly unified composition; the artist's fundamental talent is his studied skill as a craftsman; and the work of art is therefore not a window but a wall.

Cummings once phrased a definition of the poet so that the realist and formalist halves of his thought were intimately juxtaposed. "A poet," he said, "is somebody who feels, and who expresses his feeling through words." But the halves remain two rather than a single line of thought. For Cummings, art had referential and formal or relational dimensions of meaning; but nowhere was he clear about the relationship between them. Significantly, this unresolved dualism in Cummings' esthetics paralleled other dualisms in his thinking. Cummings was, for example, at odds with himself about the fundamental nature of man. Man is, like a penguin, two selves. He is both an awkward waddler and a graceful swimmer. The swimming penguin symbolizes "each human being's second, inner, or *unconscious* self," and this unconscious self is the "function which determines or fulfills each human being's destiny and which contains the essence or meaning of all destiny." That is, despite the inadequacy of most people's daily lives, a meaningful existence of love and beauty and joy is always and immediately available.

But Cummings concluded his reflections on men and penguins

with symptomatic illogic: "Not only does the Unconscious exist—
it *is* existence: and moreover, the best part of existence. . . ."[13]
In one sense, Cummings repeated here his most characteristic
theme. There is a false mode of living and a genuine one. There
is the self one sees when he looks in the mirror and a real self.
The mirror self worships bathtubs; the real self worships life.
This sense of a genuine, as distinct from the average, existence
formed the basis for Cummings' repeated invitations to people
to change their lives. It was the basis for his anger toward
most people: scientists, businessmen, generals, politicians, and
Cambridge ladies—all the people who would shoot elephants to
make billiard balls. These people are out of touch with the
genuine. But Cummings was never simple-minded, and he recognized the absolute impossibility of human beings living always
and totally in the domain of the real. This honest recognition of
human limitation was what forced the logically damaging qualification, "and moreover, *the best part* of existence."

If genuine existence is merely a walk into the next room and
if most men simply fail to realize how easy it is to open the
door and walk in, then Cummings might legitimately have characterized this other room as the whole of real existence. If, on
the other hand, the door is locked and men can hope to pass
through it on only rare occasions in a lifetime, then Cummings
did not properly call it the whole, but rather a peculiarly important, "best part" of existence. Logically, it is clear, the inner self
cannot be both the whole of genuine existence and merely a part
of it. Fundamentally, however, Cummings' unresolved problem
was that, despite his certainty that human fulfillment is perpe-
tually possible, he both believed and doubted that man could
achieve that fulfillment by himself. He believed that man can
become a swimming penguin by an exercise of will, but he also
believed that such a change requires superhuman grace.

This dualism in Cummings' conception of man paralleled, in
turn, a contrasting pair of poetic settings to which the poet
returned repeatedly. One side of Cummings produced poems of
sunrise, daylight, springtime, and childhood. The emphasis fell
on putting aside convention and receiving the varied, concrete
sense-data of the perceivable world. But another side made a
surprising number of poems about twilight, nighttime, darkness,
and death. The emphasis in these poems fell on putting aside the

sensuously perceivable and receiving intimations of the spiritual essence of things. The first insisted on the primacy of individual self-consciousness in contrast to social and intellectual conformity; the second, on the primacy of self-denial in contrast to self-consciousness.

These philosophical problems were, of course, not peculiar to Cummings. The history of Christianity could easily be written in terms of its various efforts to front a series of insoluble dilemmas concerning the nature of God, man, society, and history. Particularly during the twentieth century, philosophers such as Alfred North Whitehead and Bertrand Russell have tried to decide whether scientific knowledge stems from inferences about a knowable world or whether it is a series of hypothetical constructions about a reality that is basically beyond human reach. When, for example, we say we know that the stick which is half submerged in water is "really" straight even though it appears bent, it is difficult to determine whether our knowledge depends on some correspondence between the concept "straight stick" and the real world, or whether it depends finally on a coherent relationship between the idea of a straight stick and our desire to believe in a stable universe plus such other ideas as the refraction of light waves.

If there is a significant difference between the contradictions in Cummings' thinking and the similar contradictions in science, philosophy, and religion, it is that Cummings was less conscious of them than the residents of the more intellective worlds. In this, however, he was one with other artists. It is worth recalling a portion of Whistler's famous comment about the portrait of his mother. The artist, he said, should do more than imitate; he should "paint the man, in short, as well as his features; in arrangement of colours to treat a flower as his key, not as his model." The statement as a whole is, of course, a manifesto of pure formalism. The idea of painting "the man . . . as well as his features," on the other hand, is merely to value a deep realism over a superficial realism. Whistler shared Cummings' confusion about the referential and formal elements of art.

But if Cummings' esthetics were not coherent, there is a better explanation available than the mere fact that other artists have been similarly guilty. In the first place, the realism-formalism conflict *is* insoluble. The referential and relational dimensions of meaning are part of the nature of things. Words, colors, shapes, and notes are inevitably associated in human experience with the world beyond. That they refer to many things, often in complicated ways, is both the possibility and the necessity for art. At the same time, however, meaning depends also on the relation among words or notes when arranged in a particular context. A low note played by a tuba may have meaning partly because it is associated with a fog horn or a human groan, but its meaning depends also on the notes that precede and follow it and the notes played simultaneously with it.

A second reason for the contradiction at the heart of Cummings' esthetics may be apparent from the preceding paragraph. That words both point to things and relate to other words is so obvious that only philosophers need worry about it—certainly not practicing poets. This is clearly the reason why Cummings was able to say so casually that a poet "is somebody who feels, and who expresses his feeling through words." If the double-faceted character of art is obvious, however, it has not always been so, nor even is it obvious to everyone today. Realists in the nineteenth century thought they were saying something significant when they said they were trying to capture nature as it actually is, without regard to empty artistic formalisms.[14] Cummings certainly thought he was making a significant distinction when he said that the Cubist painters "use design to express their personal reaction to the subject." And indeed, historically speaking, what they said was important. Their words reflect, even if not neatly and directly, the emphases of their art. Furthermore, Cummings' keen but unreconciled awareness of both dimensions of his art may have been precisely what made him such a tireless experimenter. If he had been less conscious of them he would have been a less interesting and important poet; if he had been more conscious of them, he might have become a professional philosopher.

Ultimately, however, the most persuasive explanation of Cummings' failure to face the conflict between the esthetics of realism and of formalism is that his central esthetic concern was neither the nature nor the methods of art but rather esthetic experience. No matter whether a work of art is primarily a crafted composition or a window on the world, the purpose of looking at it was, in Cummings' view, clear and unambiguous. In the presence of a first-rate work the viewer undergoes an apocalyptic experience and feels himself so profoundly moved that he becomes, for the moment at least, a new man. The work may force him to put aside his conventional knowledge so that he may see love or egotism or a vomiting man or a leaf falling as though for the first time. Or the work may force him to put aside his conventional interest in subject matter so that he may discover a fully realized esthetic form. In either case, the viewer is renewed. His experience provides him a new wine skin. He gives himself over to something outside of himself. This experience is, ultimately, what Cummings meant when he said that art is "a question of being alive."

CHAPTER 6

An American Poet

"What then is the American, this new man?"
—J. Hector St. John de Crèvecoeur

I *Beyond Battleships: The Immigrant's Faith*

CUMMINGS' BIOGRAPHER and friend Charles Norman tells the story of the time he read some of Robert Frost's poems to Cummings. Cummings had said to Norman, "You know, I ought to like Frost. After all, we're both New Englanders. But I've never been able to read him." Norman read aloud several selections from the four or five volumes of Frost's poetry which Cummings had in his bookshelves. Cummings listened carefully and then, after Norman had finished reading and after a thoughtful pause, he said, "Would you like to know what I think? They lack intensity."[1]

One explanation for the differences between the two poets is that Cummings' inspiration was always more national than regional. The characteristically New England penchant for laconic understatement has always distinguished Frost's poetry and has no place in Cummings'. Like a stoical Yankee farmer, Frost was born a wise old man; Cummings never ceased being young. The differences in the way each reflects his culture can be overstated, but they are nevertheless significant, for Cummings' relation to his native land supplies perspective on the unique qualities of his poetry, a perspective which complements that of his relation to twentieth-century art.

Cummings spoke with an American accent. His style was an American style. He did not try consciously to be a national poet, but he was one nevertheless. A few years ago a traveling show of totally abstract paintings impressed foreign critics as unmistakably American although many of the painters professed to be uninterested in "American" painting and although many Congressmen insisted that the show was positively unAmerican. Cummings was an American poet in the same way. He was indeed the more genuinely representative for having been relatively unconscious of his role.

At various times in American history artists in every medium have tried deliberately to infuse their work with national qualities. But composers today have little patience with the use of folk tunes or jazz idioms as the low road to American music, and poets and novelists know that more than a dash of slang and a twist of the Western prairies are necessary for an American literature. The best American artists express their understanding of man and the world. If their work is authentic enough, the mark of their nationality will be present along with the marks of other aspects of their experience, both more personal and more universal. E. E. Cummings wrote American poetry because he was a fine poet and because America was an inevitable part of his experience.

The kind of understanding of America which a poet can provide is different from opinion polls or historical research. Cummings, for example, was very far from being a typical American. Statistically speaking, he was probably as untypical as any man could possibly be. He was, however, peculiarly sensitive to his surroundings, and his poems therefore reveal something about his culture which is at once more immediate and more profound than scientific analysis and generalization. To Crèvecoeur's question about what an American is, a question which has echoed back and forth across the United States and around the world during the nearly two centuries since he first phrased it, Cummings' poetry affords an important answer. The poetry and the nation share characteristic traits, and characteristic strengths and weaknesses as well.

In a Pulitzer Prize winning history of nineteenth-century immigration, *The Uprooted*, Oscar Handlin offered his own kind of insight into the uniqueness of Cummings' America. Handlin compared the life of the European peasant with the passage to the New World and with life in the New World itself. The entire structure of peasant life served in the endless battle against a hostile environment. The highest hope for the peasant was to hold steady, to maintain himself and his family against the apparently whimsical onslaughts of taxes, wars, and famines. To grow was to struggle on more or less even terms with the forces of decay. The whole social system, focused in the twin centers, the priest and the lord of the manor, was designed for stability.

The immigrant, participant though he was in this structure of physical events, social relations, and values, was the one who nevertheless saw sufficient hope for a new life beyond the horizon to be willing to take risks to find it. He was the one who ventured beyond the village in the hope that the unknown would prove more satisfactory than the known. Somewhere in the depth of his being he hoped that growth could mean advance and expansion rather than mere maintenance and, at best, nestings against disaster.

Handlin fronted the perplexing paradox that Americans are at once very like and very unlike their European, and particularly their English, ancestors. They share a common language, common legal and political institutions, a common philosophical and religious heritage. Americans, for example, are sometimes thought to be uniquely empirical and pragmatic in their outlook. They are thought to be peculiarly suspicious of doctrines and ideologies, tough-minded about the need for concrete evidence. But England is the historic home of both philosophic and political realism. The empirical temper is at least as much English in origin as American. Handlin's narrative of the immigrant suggests an explanation for this paradox. America was peopled neither by revolutionaries, nor necessarily by the strongest, the most courageous, the most ingenious (although all of these qualities were required to survive the transplantation process). America was settled, rather, by those Europeans who believed in what Handlin calls the values of flight—that is, the largest faith that life would be better away from home.

No satisfactory explanation of American culture can avoid consideration of the continuing immigration experiences on successive Western frontiers, on the trail from farm to city, and, today, from one metropolis to another; nor the influence of economic abundance and of two insulating oceans. And yet Handlin's attention to the immigrant and to his self-conscious hope in what lay beyond the horizon remains peculiarly suggestive, for much of the temper of American history, institutions, individual psychology, and art can be understood as reproductions of the immigrant's faith in the promise of a new start.

It is the faith which motivated, for example, Frank Lloyd Wright. A dialogue with a group of British architects one evening revealed the inmost springs of Wright's sensibility with striking clarity. At the conclusion of Wright's talk, an Englishman in the audience rose to protest Wright's implication that people needed a sense of spaciousness in order to live happily. On the contrary, the Englishman argued, England's great strength is that her people had learned to live in a restricted space. "There is no better man than the Cockney soldier," he said, "and no one who can bear hardships with greater fortitude and cheerfulness. I think that is due to the fact that he has lived what I may call a battleship existence through living in crowded quarters."

Wright felt deeply challenged, and he responded passionately and eloquently. The Englishman's point of view was a negation of everything Wright believed in. He acknowledged that human life could adapt to harsh circumstances, but such adaptation was not the end of life. "Why," he asked, "did Englishmen come to the new country we call ours now? Why have we this great new nation and this new country of America?" His own interpretation, like Handlin's, was that the early settlers were unwilling to accept the Englishman's fundamental sense of life. "To be humane," Wright concluded, "we must stand for a philosophy of freedom, rather than for any philosophy of battleship existence."[2]

There in bold outline is the uniquely American faith in a freer, more open, more fully human future. It is in what Wright said and in the eloquence with which he said it. It motivates the supercharged pace of American life that consistently impresses foreigners. Americans have a characteristic impatience. Every new problem demands an immediate solution. Life must constantly be moving forward and upward. Perhaps the outstanding single illustration is American education. Despite obvious limitations on the teaching-learning process even at its best, curricula, methods, and materials are in constant flux in America, from grade school to graduate school. The basic hope is always that a modification here and a re-evaluation there will actually produce the informed, wise, adventurous, happy graduates that education has always worked for but never before achieved. Educators are too sophisticated, of course, to acknowledge openly that they are perfectionists. Indeed, most would insist that they are not. Yet the evidence of constant change and the enthusiasm for each new educational experiment mean that perfectionism is so deeply imbedded that it goes unrecognized. American educators can no more live a "battleship existence" than Frank Lloyd Wright.

The unusually high level of aspiration that shows itself in vigorous experiment and change appears even more strikingly in moments of furious immobility. That most vigorous, even rambunctious, of all men, Theodore Roosevelt, once made a revealing comment about himself—and his culture—when he said: "Black care rarely sits behind a rider whose pace is fast enough." Behind the famed vigor lay moments of anguished frustration, so that the current of his life and, perhaps, of American life in general, is actually an alternation between activity and passivity, both equally intense. The fundamental faith in a life of advance gives Americans an unusually low frustration quotient. It produces the pronouncements about "agonizing reappraisals," the sense of stymied helplessness common among workers on factory assembly lines, the large number of American alcoholics, as well as the embarrassing displays of temperament among American athletes.

Matthew Josephson was speaking of essentially the same impulse when he noted of American literature, "An obsession with evil, early sorrow, and death appears astonishingly native to the American muse." Few people feel the effects of failure as deeply as the American because few have such a deep expectation of success. What is distinctively American about this sense of life's promise is not the idea of promise as such, nor even the secular character of the idea—the notion, that is, that fulfillment is possible tomorrow if one applies the right combination of intelligence and effort. Both of these are common possessions of the entire post-Renaissance, Western world. What is distinctively American is not that Americans believe the promised land to be just over the horizon, but rather that they have believed it so fervently and so long that it takes a skilled diagnostician to recognize their belief for what it is.

II *Art As Intensity*

This intensity of commitment is what the Scottish poet and critic G. S. Fraser saw in Cummings when he referred to his "permanent adolescence." In addition to being perceptive, Fraser's comment is so colorful that it deserves to be quoted at length. He said:

> Mr. Cummings' love poetry is, in a bad sense, *impersonal;* and I would connect this impersonality of the love poetry with a general characteristic of the poetry as a whole, its steadily sustained youthful strident energy, of which the dark shadow is its almost complete failure to mature. Mr. Cummings wrote in 1923 as well as he does now [1955], and not very differently. The marks of permanent adolescence in his work are many. Let me list some: 1. an almost entirely uncritical devotion to parents, lovers, and a few chosen friends combined with an attitude of suspicion and dislike toward "outsiders": 2. a general tendency to think of *all* political and economic activities as in the main a sinister conspiracy against the young: 3. a wholehearted universalistic pacifism, deeply emotional, not argued out, combined with a natural violent irascibility: 4. the instinctive generosity of youth (always side emotionally with the rioters against the police) combined with an equally deeply rooted provincial intolerance (unless I am obtuse in finding this intolerance in the dialect parodies and in some of the references to people with Jewish or German names): 5. the violent capacity of the young for disgust (recurrent references to drunkenness, vomit, and so on) which can itself, uncriticized, become disgusting: 6. a youthful, not very well-balanced religiousness, a "reverence for life" combined with a youthful refusal to accept death as a fact ("No young man thinks that he will ever die. . . ."), leading, of course, to a morbid preoccupation with death: 7. indecency, scatology, even here and there something that strikes me as very like pornography—physical frustration leading to emotional, and making even physical fulfillment finally emotionally frustrating, and final emotional fulfillment the object of a kind of private religion. To sum all this up: Mr. Cummings' sense of life is the "lyrical" rather than the

"tragic" or "comic" sense. The poet who has not learned to accept "society," "others," the idea of the City in some sense, will never become sufficiently mature for tragedy or comedy. Mr. Cummings' satire is an aggressive-defensive maneuver on behalf of his small private corner in a, for him, still unsullied Garden of Eden; . . .[3]

Fraser's review is peculiarly valuable, because he responded to Cummings much as the British architect reacted to Wright: he too felt that his whole personality, not only his esthetic values but also his entire sense of life, was challenged. As a result, his review is a kind of inverted mirror which reflects not only what is distinctively Cummings but distinctively American. Fraser was apparently aware himself that more was involved in his response than the task of book reviewing, narrowly conceived, for he concluded his evaluation by saying, "A society gets the poets it deserves, and America has obviously deserved very well to get a poet of the painful, raw honesty of Mr. Cummings." Fraser recognized, that is, that his measuring stick had been the restrained dignity appropriate to a "battleship existence." Half-consciously, he had searched Cummings in vain for the maturity and strength of character which the British have always prized in the gentleman. Finally, however, he had to acknowledge also that, granting America's different tone of life, Cummings wrote with appropriate eloquence. In some details Fraser is simply mistaken, as he is when he suggests that Cummings never accepted the idea of the city. Yet, taken as a whole, Fraser's review usefully points to Cummings' American accent, for it is with a special intensity that Cummings fulfilled the dual role of critic and of celebrant of his native land.

The raw honesty that Fraser cited refers to Cummings' relation to both his material and his readers. He was talking about Cummings' unwillingness ever to accept any artistic task as simple. Never did Cummings merely write a poem. He accepted neither springtime, nor roses, nor human relationships, nor the stars as they first appeared to him. Nor did he accept instinctively the language inherited from his culture. Rather, with a fervent concentration, he searched for new experience and new meaning, particularly in the life which was closest to hand. He did so because his particular version of the American faith was that life is far more world-shatteringly valuable than even he—most of the time—fully realized. In turn, having made some new discovery about trees or elephants or love, he could not take it for granted that his experience would be easily communicated to others.

One critic has said that Cummings used strange typography because he did not trust his readers, and, in a very real sense, he is right.[4] Cummings shared with the modern movement in all the arts and with the American tradition in literature the fear that audiences would bring with them the wrong attitude toward art and therefore inadequate attention. Thoreau apologized to readers of *Walden* because they would have to face certain difficulties in their reading, and he tried to assure them that the problem was not his desire to be obtuse but rather the nature of the experience to be communicated. They would simply have to stand on tiptoes to read.

Basically, the difficulty in reading *Walden* is that Thoreau had undergone a profound spiritual renewal, and he was satisfied with nothing less than a book which might induce readers to share the same experience. Melville's *Moby Dick* was a similar enterprise. To readers of that most puzzling of books, Melville confessed that there were some subjects which demanded unique, even if disorderly, treatment. In his late years Henry James tried repeatedly to place his readers in a position where they would genuinely participate in the hero's progress from confusion to knowledge. This is the James that has frequently been criticized for deliberate obfuscation. His aim, however, was fundamentally the same as the most characteristic American poets and novelists from Thoreau to Cummings. Far from wanting to be precious or obscure, he hoped to shake readers from their expectation of being *merely* entertained, of *merely* reading a book, into a readiness to participate with their whole beings in a deep encounter with life itself. This is one of the main effects also of William Faulkner's decision to begin his two greatest novels, *The Sound and the Fury* and *Absalom, Absalom!*, by confronting the reader with the consciousness of, respectively, an idiot and a madwoman. The reader finds his expectations about novels and life and the way men communicate with one another completely frustrated. He is forced, as it were, to make a new start, in order that, when he is finished, he will, with a peculiar intensity, have known life as he never knew it before.

The American accent in literature then results primarily from the American writers' especially intense desire to search out anew the meaning of their experience and then to communicate with their readers in such a way that they are encouraged, if not forced, to participate. As Leo Marx said several years ago, in talking about the function of colloquial speech in American literature, American writers habitually try to escape the traditional poet-reader relationship.[5] Walt Whitman was openly insistent that his poetry be accepted as a live human being whispering lovingly across the barriers of time and space to each individual reader. But this aim was also implicit in Whitman's diction, syntax, and form, in the very fabric of his poems. By contrast, Wordsworth once embodied the overwhelming experience of discovering in London the open clarity, powerful energy, and almost supernatural serenity which he had always associated with nature, in a sonnet—the justly famous "Composed upon Westminster Bridge, September 3, 1802." It is inconceivable that Whitman could have entrusted such an experience to a sonnet, a traditional structure which, beyond all others, immediately announces, "Reader, you are about to read a poem."

Cummings and other American writers have, of course, written sonnets. But, in so doing, Cummings always managed somehow to declare that his were sonnets with a difference.[6] Generally speaking, his aim in writing sonnets was to see how untraditionally he could behave with a traditional form. His fundamental aim was, with Whitman, to establish a new relationship with the reader. And this aim reflected his sense of urgency about the importance of what he had to say.

In this sense, Cummings celebrated America with far greater effect than the Fourth of July oratory that he took such delight in satirizing. He gave artistic form to that deep and urgent faith in life's promise which is recognized the world over as peculiarly American—whether that faith wears the mask of prison reforms, a popular song about love being a many splendored thing, a Congressman's effort to write a law covering every administrative eventuality, a businessman's energetic efficiency, or the automobile tail-fin (the tail-fin's very meretriciousness reflects an insatiable desire for progress: if technological advance is unavailable, a hollow stylistic frill is more acceptable than no change at all).

III *"Human Souls Positively Cannot Be Drycleaned"*

But Cummings' participation in the basic temper of American life did not, by any means, lead him to accept uncritically all of its surface manifestations. He did, to be sure, reject, what he felt was merely snobbish criticism of American life. In 1927, for example, when France was the rage for expatriate artists and vacationing executives, Cummings wrote an article for *Vanity Fair* praising America for her size. His native land, he said, had the intensity which accompanies size—particularly, necessary, organic size. Marin, Lachaise, and Niagara Falls, he said, are America's answers to Chartres, Notre Dame, and the Louvre: they represent that central aspect of America which is "happening" rather than "happened." America "may be going to Hell, of course," he concluded, "but at least she isn't standing still."[7] There is a kind of irresponsibility about this comment. In the large context of Cummings' thought and attitudes, however, it was implicit criticism as well as praise.

Like others in the dominant American tradition of letters, Cummings tried to capture America's capacity for belief and reorient it, to turn it from secular to transcendent values, from the merely human to the ultimately human. This is not a matter of doctrine; it is a matter simply of the locus of value, of whether today is primarily the prelude to tomorrow or whether today is valuable in its own right. The American writer has felt himself faced with a future-oriented society. He has responded by emphasizing a transcendent realm of being which exists in the present. W. H. Auden suggested the basic distinction in a brilliant comment he once made about the function of money in America.

> In the States, money, which is thought of as something you extract in your battle with the dragon of nature, represents a proof of your manhood. . . . the danger in America is anxiety because, since this quantitative thing of money is regarded as a proof of your manhood, and to make a little more of it would make you even more manly, it becomes difficult to know where to stop. This ties up with something that always annoys me: when I see Europeans accusing

Americans of being materialists. The real truth about Americans is they do not care about matter enough.[8]

As Auden pointed out, this endless American anxiety is one of the main differences between Huckleberry Finn and Oliver Twist, his English counterpart. Oliver is content finally to be taken in by Mr. Brownlow. But Huck's higher and more personal standard of value leads to a perpetual search for the right home, a search which is just being renewed as his novel ends. Melville's Captain Ahab, James' Isabel Archer, Hemingway's Lt. Henry, Fitzgerald's Jay Gatsby, Faulkner's Colonel Sutpen—all engage in a quest for some essentially unexamined vision of perfection; and, in the process, they lose the world. Their attention is so totally fixed upon an ideal that lies always just out of reach that they do not recognize the people and things and events immediately around them.

Cummings once summed up his own critique of American life by acknowledging that prosperity or revolution may be just around the corner, but, as he said, "human souls positively cannot be drycleaned." This comment, like many others, seems to place primary blame on what Cummings considered an undue faith in science and technology. But, as his treatment of the automobile in "she being Brand" suggests, Cummings was no more opposed ultimately to technology than Thoreau was. His prime antagonist was the secular faith that human fulfillment can be produced by human power. For most people, "a world is for them, them." The result is that they sow their "isn'ts" and reap their "sames." They cut themselves off from the ultimate truth that "you and i are incredibly alive."

The American faith is based in the hope that today's problems are solvable tomorrow. Cummings would have had it "move away still further: into now." The peculiarly American intensity of his poetry is the poet's urgent witness to the proposition that a new start is still possible but that it is to be made neither in a new place nor in a new time but here and now. His own concentration on language, as present to him as Walden Pond was to Thoreau or whaling to Melville, was a demonstration of his deepest meaning. Language, perhaps the most ordinary element in the human environment, was Cummings' prime source of vitality and meaning.

IV *The Dark Side of Optimism: The Divided Self*

When Fraser said of Cummings that he had a lyrical rather than a tragic sense of life, that he had never learned to accept "others," he echoed a criticism that has frequently been made not only of Cummings but of Emerson, Thoreau, Whitman, Thomas Wolfe, Hart Crane, and many other American writers. At bottom it is the same complaint that William Butler Yeats made against Emerson when he said Emerson had no "vision of evil." But Cummings had far more understanding and sympathy for the ordinary human condition than Fraser seems to have recognized. Some of Cummings' best work dramatized not only an acute sense of an uncrossable gap between the real and the ideal but also the pain and loneliness and despair that attend such a recognition. The poem "nothing is more exactly terrible" suggests, for example, that the lust for living that Cummings would ordinarily have had people substitute for problem solving can itself be destructive.

> nothing is more exactly terrible than
> to be alone in the house,with somebody and
> with something)
> > You are gone.   there is laughter
>
> and despair impersonates a street
>
> i lean from the window,behold ghosts,
> > > a man
> hugging a woman in a park.   Complete.
>
> and slightly(why?or lest we understand)
> slightly i am hearing somebody
> coming up stairs,carefully
> (carefully climbing carpeted flight after
> carpeted flight.   in stillness,climbing
> the carpeted stairs of terror)
>
> and continually i am seeing something
>
> inhaling gently a cigarette(in a mirror
> > > [*Poems 1923-1954*, p. 269]

A sense of dispossession permeates the poem. Everywhere

there is unreconcilable separation. The speaker has lost the "you" of the poem. He senses his isolation from the love and laughter in the park across the street. The fundamental dualism in the poem, however, is between the two conflicting selves of the speaker himself—the self that anxiously hopes for some slight evidence that love and fulfillment may soon return and the self that smokes cigarettes in boredom and despair. And the speaker projects this inward dualism on what he sees outside his window. The street, he feels, is merely an actor's mask being worn by despair. The park lovers are merely ghosts.

The denouement of the poem is the revelation that throughout the whole poem (or at least the second half of it) the speaker has been staring at himself in the mirror. The impact of this revelation—Fraser to the contrary notwithstanding—is the speaker's tragic discovery that, while pain and despair are functions of his very hopes and anticipations, they are nevertheless real. The poem ends in knowledge but not in lyric reconciliation.

Another poem, "but being not amazing:without love," shows not only Cummings' concern for "others" but perhaps even his concern for that "other Cummings" whom Fraser and Cummings both find immaturely narrow and unsympathetic.

> but being not amazing:without love
> separate,smileless—merely imagine your
>
> sorrow a certain reckoning demands . . .
>
> marvelling And what may have become of
> with his gradual acute lusting glance
> an alert clumsily foolishwise
>
> (tracking the beast Tomorrow by her spoor)
> over the earth wandering hunter whom you
> knew once?
>
>   what if(merely suppose)
>
> mine should overhear and answer Who
> with the useless flanks and cringing feet
> is this(shivering pale naked very poor)
> creature of shadow,that among first light
>
> groping washes my nightmare from his eyes?
>   [*Poems 1923-1954*, pp. 268-69]

The listener is not an unusual person and is therefore isolated and unhappy like the cigarette-smoking mirror-watcher of "nothing is more exactly terrible." The speaker, at the beginning of the poem, poses the prospect of a day of reckoning on which the listener will suffer for his lovelessness. The speaker, standing as he does in completely self-assured judgment of his listener, is extraordinarily like the Cummings of "a salesman is an it that stinks"; he is the harsh, angry critic of mediocrity.

The development of the poem provides interesting insight into the depth of Cummings' understanding of a poet-prophet's relation to the average man in his audience. During the hiatus at the end of line three the listener apparently imagines the true, "nightmare" character of his situation as the speaker has instructed him. The result is his utter transformation. Of primary significance is that his change from an "earth wandering hunter" to a "creature of shadow" amazes the speaker, and his amazement reflects the fraudulence of his initial prophecy. His amazement, that is, suggests that the speaker had not really believed in the possibility of the listener's resurrection. And when he realizes that it has occurred before his very eyes, he sees the awful hollowness of his own initial posture; and then wonders, with a delicate combination of fear and hope, whether his own imagination might "overhear and answer" the listener's and undergo a comparable change. The action of the poem is rendered largely through indirection, through the intensity of the speaker's unbelieving, inarticulate reaction to something which is not explicitly stated but which obviously takes place between the third and fourth lines.

This indirection produces some ambiguity concerning the nature of the listener's transformation and the speaker's reaction. It is not entirely clear whether the speaker is fearfully watching the total destruction of a personality or whether the "useless flanks and cringing feet" are signs of an outward defeat which is an inner triumph. It is even possible that the "creature of shadow," referred to in the last sentence, is the speaker himself, who, after conceiving the need and possibility of his own transformation, undergoes a change himself. What is clear is that the speaker has participated in a momentous experience. He has discovered an awesome gap between what he thought he believed and what he really believes, and the experience has severely shaken his confidence in the role of apostle.

The idea of the divided self contains the potential for both tragedy and comedy, based as it is on a serious, unblinking recognition of human insufficiency. It is not a major emphasis in Cummings' poetry, but it is present not only in his poems but in such other works as the play *Him* and even a pen-and-ink self-portrait which shows the poet in the act of removing a mask.

V *Always and Irrevocably Himself*

If life was not always black and white in Cummings created universe, if the poet was sometimes "maturely" aware of complexity and of apparently ineradicable darkness, it is nevertheless true that he nowhere evidenced the developing vision that has characterized the work of, say, T. S. Eliot. Cummings did not have to struggle through the Valley of Despond to the Celestial City. He was born there. He did not pass through a series of clearly demarked periods of technical development. Close statistical analysis has disclosed some shifts of emphasis,[9] but none is in any way comparable to the distinctions that mark a Picasso's movement from "blue period" to "pink period" to analytical cubism to synthetic cubism. Nor was there any clear rise and decline of power such as marked the careers of Melville and Faulkner. Good and bad poems appeared in each of Cummings' successive publications. As in Whitman's case, there is some temptation to find a deepening wisdom as the poet aged, and the temptation is encouraged by the large number of poems in Cummings' last volume, *95 Poems*, on the subject of death. But the large issues of life and death were central to the vocabulary of both Whitman and Cummings from their earliest work, and the excellence with which these subjects were handled bears little relation to age.

Indeed, the remarkable thing about Cummings' career was the intensely concentrated way in which he sought new subjects and new modes of expression to render essentially a single theme. To borrow his own language, he remained always and irrevocably himself. The pliancy of his single-mindedness permitted exploration of an extraordinary range of people, human situations, current events, intellectual developments, and social institutions. He returned always, of course, to life and death, love and loneliness, and the natural world—what artist of importance does not? Meanwhile, however, he spoke of poetry and prostitution, churches, business, diapers and winter sports, democracy and communism, foreign travel, zoo animals, burlesque comics and jazz pianists, Freud and Einstein, cement mixing, and high society.

In addition to range of subject matter, and perhaps more important, Cummings' poems are cast in a great variety of tones. He wrote in sorrow and anger, in tender love and tough sarcasm, in lyric celebration and casual gaiety, in quiet invitation and wild exuberance. Whatever attitude or combination of attitudes he adopted, Cummings' American intensity is almost always recognizable—even when he wrote nonsense. One of the several "essays" in *By E. E. Cummings* (1930) begins:

> Taking a sealion out of a watermelon he first deposited it in the goldfishbowl bottomsideup, causing an explosion which changed the color of everyone's eybrows, and next, to the delight of all present, caused an angleworm to appear on the janitor'sinstep, but guffaws fairly rang out when seven sixhundred pound fairies began coming five by five slowly out of the graphophone horn, waving furiously the Stars and Stripes and chewing collosal homemade whisperless mincepies.

The intensity here lies in the extreme juxtaposition of sense and nonsense. The passage has a large, dreamlike meaninglessness. It suggests at once Salvador Dali and Mark Twain and, more clearly, a Rube Goldberg machine which—with two motors, fifteen belts and wheels, a trained seal, a talking bird, a child's slide, a giant crane, and a semi-automatic brick layer—pours one small glass of water. The chain of events is totally implausible, and yet the very conventional sentence structure and vocabulary imply a serious, logical straight-faced narrator. Like much of the poetry, the passage presents an extreme challenge to the reader's ordinary commitment to logic and order and coherence.

The concentrated focus of Cummings' lifelong passion was responsible for some of his weaknesses as well as his strengths. Cummings wrote few mediocre poems. He often wrote before he was ready, but he was never willing to settle simply for a "well-made" poem. He always sought perfection. Sometimes he relied too heavily on favorite superlatives, like "illimitable" and "incalculable," as though the simple announcement of the words had magical powers. The result is a species of inarticulate and ineffective shouting at the reader. Sometimes the fragmentation of words produces no more than unconventionality, and the result is what might be called "conventional Cummings." Some poems capture a snatch of, perhaps, barroom conversation without communicating any sense of significance. These poems are realistic but unimportant. Occasional poems are downright offensive, such as "Humanity i love you" or "exit a kind of unkindness exit." The former cannot even sustain the tone of bitter sarcasm and ends bluntly, "Humanity/ i hate you." The latter, tastelessly, celebrates the death of a businessman. Neither is the work of an artist but rather of a man whose eye had momentarily turned inward and found there a raging hatred.

The success of some poets depends on their willingness to accept themselves as second rate. They work within their powers and produce some eminently satisfying verse. Always poised and controlled, they do not violate the canons of good taste. By contrast, Cummings always took risks in his writing. His choice of subjects and his fundamental attitude toward life made him constantly liable to sentimental excess. But this is a risk that first-rate artists always run. It is certainly the risk that is forced upon a religious poet in twentieth-century America.

In a nation which is, generally speaking, comfortable, proud of its accomplishments, and convinced that progress is a basic condition of life and which sees pain and failure and confusion as problems essentially of technology—in this world a poet who believes deeply in the insufficiency of man and the Grace of God must take desperate measures. Mature people, even mature believers, know that "I-Thou" experiences are rare; and they place high value on resignation and restraint and dignity. The worst of sins, they would say, with Robert Frost, is to make a fuss. Cummings, on the other hand, devoted his life to the prophetic vision of both the immediate and ultimate reality of love. This vision placed him in opposition to most of his countrymen. But the intensity of his commitment was their intensity. And the hope that his readers would one day be persuaded—the hope which motivated his ceaseless experimentation—was their hope.

The urgency in his poetic voice is, in short, their urgency. Cummings was one of a continuous line of American artists who have challenged the nation to reassess fundamental aims and values. But the nation itself supplied the passion and the persistence that have permeated that challenge. Cummings' poetry is one long letter, pregnant with joy, addressed to most people from an immigrant in nowhere.

Notes and References

Chapter One

1. This poem, like several others by Cummings, is a visual poem. It cannot be read aloud. Comments about the poem's sounds, therefore, presuppose the working of an "inner ear." See analysis of "Among these red pieces of day," especially p. 29.

2. See Norman Friedman's analysis of this poem in his *E. E. Cummings: The Art of His Poetry* (Baltimore, 1960), pp. 171-72.

3. William Carlos Williams, "E. E. Cummings' Paintings and Poems," *Arts Digest*, XXIX (December 1, 1954), 7-8.

4. For a contrary approach and interpretation concerning "nonsun blob," see Friedman, pp. 108-10.

5. Th. Van de Velde, *Ideal Marriage* (London, 1928), p. 249.

6. Other readings of "Among these red pieces of day" appear in: John Peale Bishop, "The Poems and Prose of E. E. Cummings," *The Southern Review*, IV (Summer, 1938), 176-77; Laura Riding and Robert Graves, *A Survey of Modernist Poetry* (London, 1929), pp. 84ff; Edith Sitwell, *Aspects of Modern Poetry* (London, 1934). pp. 256-57.

7. See also Herbert C. Barrows, Jr. and William R. Steinhoff, *The Explicator*, IX (October, 1950), 1 and George W. Sullivan, "The Poems of E. E. Cummings," unpublished master's thesis, Brown University, 1949, pp. 63ff.

Chapter Two

1. I am heavily indebted to Robert L. Beloof's insights concerning this poem. See his unpublished doctoral dissertation, "E. E. Cummings: The Prosodic Shape of His Poems," Northwestern University, 1954, pp. 44ff.

2. George J. Firmage (ed.), *E. E. Cummings: A Miscellany* (New York, 1958), pp. 189-92.

3. *Ibid.*, p. 46.

Chapter Three

1. E. E. Cummings, *Eimi* (New York, 1933), p. 319.

2. Raoul de Roussy de Sales, "Love in America," *Atlantic Monthly*, CLXI (May, 1938), 645-51.

3. See, for example, Theodore Spencer, "Technique as Joy," *Harvard Wake*, I (Spring, 1946), 25-26.

4. Erich Fromm, *The Art of Loving* (New York, 1956), pp. 87-88.

5. There is a sense in which, in the first stanza, the speaker asserts strength rather than impotence. He is saying, "Of course, I don't have the strength of God, but I'm a lot stronger than most men." The second stanza, however, clearly implies that, prior to the beginning of the poem, the speaker and his lover have discovered and have been talking about "my weakness." However elusive and ambiguous the first stanza is, the speaker must at least be seen in a defensive posture.

Chapter Four

1. Indeed Cummings accepted the seriousness of his graduation assignment so fully that he even agreed to certain editorial revisions recommended by his father. Cummings' classmate S. Foster Damon recalls that Cummings had originally intended to refer to Duchamp's "Nude Descending a Staircase," which the two had seen together when the Armory Show traveled to Boston in 1913, as a "phallic phantasy." At the last minute, however, Cummings permitted his father to dissuade him from such an offense against decency. (Letter from Damon to the author.)

2. Firmage, pp. 23-33.

3. *Ibid.*, pp. 34-37.

4. *Ibid.*, pp. 38-44.

5. *Ibid.*, p. 74.

6. *Ibid.*, p. 47.

7. *Ibid.*, pp. 93-94.

8. *Ibid.*, p. 220.

9. See, for example, *ibid.*, p. 9.

10. *Ibid.*, p. 69.

11. *Ibid.*, pp. 7-8.

12. Wassily Kandinsky. *The Art of Spiritual Harmony* (London, 1914), pp. 21, 37.

13. Albert Gleizes and Jean Metzinger, *Cubism* (London, 1913), p. 51.

14. Quoted in Joseph Kwiat, "Robert Henri and the Emerson-Whitman Tradition," *Publications of the Modern Language Association*, LXXI (September, 1956), 620.

15. Cummings, *Eimi*, p. 25.

16. Firmage, p. 7.

17. *Ibid.*, p. 11.

18. Rudolph Von Abele has systematically and exhaustively classified Cummings' techniques in his article " 'Only to Grow': Change in the Poetry of E. E. Cummings," *Publications of the Modern Language Association,* LXX (December, 1955), 913-33.

19. Quoted in MacKinley Helm, *John Marin* (Boston, 1948), p. 8.

20. In 1952 Cummings told a critic that he uses capitalization as a way simply to break up the way a poem "falls" on the page. See Beloof, p. 67.

Chapter Five

1. The clearest and most comprehensive, single statement of Poe's esthetic principles is his review of Nathaniel Hawthorne's *Twice Told Tales.*

2. James A. McNeill Whistler, *Ten O'Clock* (Portland. Me., 1925), pp. 34-35.

3. The closest approximation in literature is the new critics' concept of poetry's "autonomy." But the new critics meant, primarily, that previous criticism had treated literature too exclusively in terms of literary movements, social milieu, and authors' personal lives. Their intent was to deny the relevance of literature's origin to meaning; they have never denied that literature *has* meanings. In practice, new critics have characteristically emphasized complexity of meaning rather than lack of it.

4. Clive Bell, *Art* (New York, 1930 [1913]), pp. 12, 70-71, 291-92.

5. Firmage, pp. 17-22.

6. *Ibid.,* pp. 34-37.

7. Cummings, *Eimi,* p. 58.

8. Firmage, p. 65.

9. *Ibid.,* pp. 67-68.

10. Bishop, p. 178.

11. The following self-explanatory lines from Alexander Pope's "Essay on Criticism" constitute the most famous single illustration of the role of time in poetry:

> "When Ajax strives some rock's vast weight to throw,
> The line too labors and the words move slow;
> Not so, when swift Camilla scours the plain,
> Flies o'er the unbending corn, and skims along the main."

12. R. P. Blackmur, "Notes on E. E. Cummings' Language," *Hound and Horn,* IV (January-March, 1931), 163-92; reprinted in Blackmur's *Language as Gesture* (New York, 1952), and also in his *Form and Value in Modern Poetry* (New York, 1957).

13. Firmage, pp. 50-53.

14. E. H. Gombich's *Art and Illusion* (New York, 1960), Chapter 1 demonstrates that the most careful effort to imitate nature must finally depend on the relationships on a painting's surface. Nature's tonal values are too complex for it to be otherwise.

Chapter Six

1. Charles Norman, *The Magic-Maker* (New York, 1958), p. 186.
2. Frank Lloyd Wright, *An Organic Architecture* (London, 1939), pp. 31-33.
3. G. S. Fraser, "The Aesthete and the Sensationalist," *Partisan Review*, XXII (Spring, 1955), 267-68.
4. Sullivan, pp. 99-100.
5. Leo Marx, "The Vernacular Tradition in American Literature" in Joseph Kwiat and Mary Turpie (eds.), *Studies in American Culture* (Minneapolis, 1960), pp. 109-22.
6. See, for example, "life?" quoted in full on p. 73.
7. Firmage, pp. 97-98.
8. W. H. Auden, "Huck and Oliver" in Leslie Fiedler (ed.), *The Art of the Essay* (New York, 1958), p. 602.
9. See Von Abele's study in *PMLA*, cited above.

Selected Bibliography

PRIMARY SOURCES

The Enormous Room. New York: Boni and Liveright, 1922. Also:
New York: The Modern Library, 1934.
Tulips and Chimneys. New York: Thomas Seltzer, 1923.
& (And). New York: Privately Printed, 1925.
XLI Poems. New York: The Dial Press, 1925.
Is 5. New York: Boni and Liveright, 1926.
Him. New York: Boni and Liveright, 1927.
CIOPW. New York: Covici, Friede, 1931.
VV (ViVa). New York: Horace Liveright, 1931.
Eimi. New York: Covici, Friede, 1933. Also: New York: Grove Press,
1958.
No Thanks. Mount Vernon, N. Y.: The Golden Eagle Press, 1935.
Collected Poems. New York: Harcourt, Brace, 1938.
50 Poems. New York: Duell, Sloan, and Pearce, 1940.
1 x 1. New York: Henry Holt, 1944.
XAIPE. New York: Oxford University Press, 1950.
i: Six Nonlectures. Cambridge: Harvard University Press, 1953.
Poems 1923-1954. New York: Harcourt, Brace, 1954.
E. E. Cummings: A Miscellany. New York: Argophile Press, 1958.
95 Poems. New York: Harcourt, Brace, 1958.
See also George J. Firmage, *E. E. Cummings: A Bibliography.* Middle-
town: Wesleyan University Press, 1960.

SECONDARY SOURCES

BAUM, S. V. "E. E. Cummings: The Technique of Immediacy," *South
Atlantic Quarterly,* LIII (January, 1954), 70-88. Valuable particularly for the interpretation of individual poems.
BISHOP, JOHN PEALE. "The Poetry and Prose of E. E. Cummings,"
The Southern Review, IV (Summer, 1938), 173-86. A somewhat
inconclusive but nevertheless wide-ranging, shrewd, and balanced
judgment, rendered with the special authority of a poet and a
contemporary of Cummings.

E. E. CUMMINGS

BLACKMUR, RICHARD P. *Language as Gesture*. New York: Harcourt, Brace, 1952. The essay, "Notes on E. E. Cummings' Language," is a distinguished statement which accuses Cummings of being a romantic egoist, a sentimental antagonist of intelligence, and therefore unintelligible.

FINCH, JOHN. "New England Prodigal," *New England Quarterly*, XII (December, 1939), 643-53. A thoughtful rejection of Cummings' romanticism, in its political (broadly speaking) as well as its poetic dimensions.

FRIEDMAN, NORMAN. *E. E. Cummings: The Art of His Poetry*. Baltimore: The Johns Hopkins Press, 1960. This first full-length critical study tends toward the encyclopedic, but it is sensitive, well informed, and persuasive. The two chapters entitled "Action" and "Creation" are exceptionally valuable. The latter is based on painstaking study of 175 pages of Cummings' notes for what became, finally, a nine-stanza poem.

HAINES, GEORGE. "::2:1 The World and E. E. Cummings," *Sewanee Review*, LIX (Spring, 1951), 206-27. Haines is unduly insistent upon Cummings' "new authority" after *Eimi*. His article as a whole is the best single essay on Cummings' poetry to date. Contains a brilliant reading of the poem "mortals)."

HARVARD WAKE, I (Spring, 1946). Essayists in this "Cummings number" include William Carlos Williams, Paul Rosenfeld, Lionel Trilling. With the exception of Theodore Spencer's "Technique as Joy," the articles reveal less about *Cummings* than about the authors themselves. As a group, however, they provide invaluable insight into Cummings' contemporary reputation.

MONROE, HARRIET. "Flare and Blare," *Poetry*, XXIII (January, 1924), 211-15. This review essay concerning *Tulips and Chimneys* is interesting primarily as the first reaction of a highly influential person in the world of poetry. Monroe rejected Cummings' experimental typography as a merely irrelevant eccentricity but responded sensitively to the large purposes of his art.

NORMAN, CHARLES. *The Magic-Maker*. New York: The Macmillan Company, 1958. Indispensable biography, written in sprightly prose by a friend of the poet.

RIDING, LAURA AND ROBERT GRAVES. *A Survey of Modernist Poetry*. London: William Heinemann, Ltd., 1929. Cummings and T. S. Eliot are the twin centers of this early but still useful study.

VON ABELE, RUDOLPH. "'Only to Grow': Change in the Poetry of E. E. Cummings," *Publications of the Modern Language Association*, LXX (December, 1955), 913-33. A thoroughly systematic treatment of Cummings' themes and techniques and their development.

Index

Index

Index